Dear Africa

Dear Africa

The Call of the African Dream

Andrew Wutawunashe

Contents

Preface ix

Chapter 1.   Being Black 3

Chapter 2.   "Im ayn anee lee, mee lee" 13
              Rabbi Hillel

Chapter 3.   The Village Icon 25

Chapter 4.   *"Die Religion ist das opium des Volkes . . . ,"* 51
              Karl Marx, 1844.

Chapter 5.   The Ultimate Weapon 63

Chapter 6.   Sights and Sounds 85

Chapter 7.   African Patriots 113

Chapter 8.   The New Leader 125

Chapter 9.   Dear Africa, ... 139

Chapter 10.   Hear this Dream 147

Acknowledgements 161

Dedication

*Dedicated to those men, women and children who gave
their lives for the emancipation, freedom, dignity and self-
determination of Black People everywhere. May their Dream live
in the hearts of generation after generation, and bring upward
change to the face of Africa and Black People everywhere.*

Preface

I hope you are one of those enlightened people who are concerned about the state of the Black people, people of African origin who are both on the African Continent and in all nations of the world. It is with reference to this people that the term "Africa" or "African" is used throughout this book. The author acknowledges that there are people of other colours, historical background or other immigrants who qualify for the term "African" by reason of descent or by reason of a choice to make this beautiful Continent their home. However, it is common cause that the overwhelming majority of people who are today inhabitants of the continent of Africa and whose progenitors are the acknowledged indigenous owners of Africa, are the Black people. The state of Black people both on and outside the Continent of Africa continues to be a matter of great concern. Crime ravages disadvantaged Black communities. The grim spectre of poverty and economic deprivation appears to persistently overshadow Black people's lives wherever they are. Political confusion plagues various African nations and often results in endemic social strife and civil wars. Divisions are chronic, and unity, including the uniting of the African Continent, is a long overdue, yet indispensable goal for the future strength of Black people. The economic, military and political weakness of Black nations has fostered a culture of dependence which some predator nations in turn take advantage of in order to undermine the self determination of Black people. From these nations flows a relentless pontificating which appears to imply that the woes of Black people are due to their alleged monopoly of the triplet cultures of inferiority complex, incompetence and corruption.

The reality is that most of the troubles of Black people are rooted in the devastating effects of such abuses as slavery and colonialism. These abuses mothered an economic and psychological plunder of Black people from which effective tools and remedies for recovery have not yet been put into the hands of Black people. Not even the concept of Reparations or a Marshal Plan has been considered requisite for a people who endured a sustained holocaust and four hundred years of plunder at the hands of other races. It is a telling indictment of former oppressors of Black people that even today, over fifty years after Kenya's independence, Kenyans have to sue the British Government in a London High Court for compensation for numerous atrocities which included such unthinkable acts of sheer blood lust as castration of male victims in detention camps.

In occasionally chronicling some of the wrongs done to Black people, it is not the aim of this author to imprison Black people in bitterness and self-pity, nor to provide them an excuse for perpetually remaining in a place of disadvantage. To the contrary, awareness of their painful history and its far reaching effects empowers them and all who genuinely desire to partner with them on their challenging journey to their restoration by helping them to understand the root causes of their problems so as to accurately deal with them.

The rise of Black people everywhere is in the interest of the whole human race. This author believes that there is purpose and design in the diversity of nations on the face of the earth—that each people should rise to their prime and enrich all peoples with their unique contributions in various areas. This is the reason why Black people must now themselves take responsibility for their ascent among nations into a place of competitiveness. African Leaders must take every step necessary to resist any attempt by former colonial masters to reimpose a schoolboy-schoolmaster relationship. Through unity and a true belief in themselves, Black people can realise genuine self-determination.

This book is a letter to all Black people and to those who choose to be their partners, to help them to understand the strategic areas that need to be dealt with for the rise of Black people. Often we believe it is material things that if put in our hands will cause us to rise. To the contrary, you will learn in this book that the resources needed for the rise of the Black people are for the most part abstract and are already within us. This book is required reading for every Black man, woman and child. It is also an important book which all leaders of Black people—political, social, educational, business, religious—indeed leaders in every area—cannot afford to ignore. It is indeed, a personal letter to you.

Ambassador Jonathan Wutawunashe,
MA International Relations, American University

Chapter 1

"I have a dream . . . ." On 28 August 1963 in Washington, DC., Rev. Dr. Martin Luther King Jr. shared a Dream which inspired Black people to fight for their rights in America and beyond.

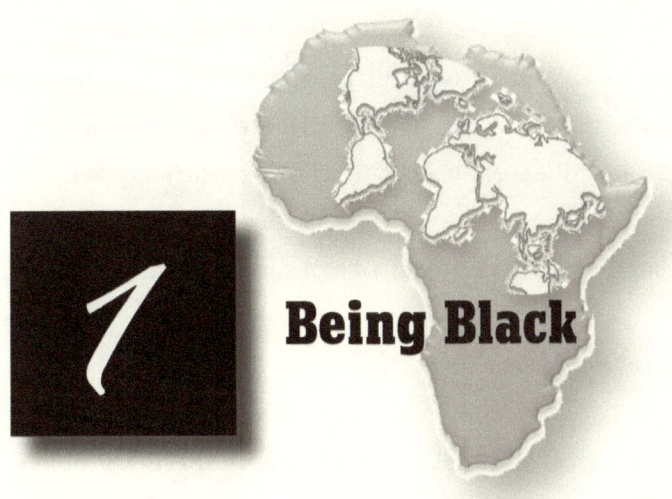

Being Black

I *have a dream . . . that one day my four children will not be judged by the colour of their skin, but by the content of their character . . . .*

Rev. Dr. Martin Luther King Jr.

Being Black is an issue.

*T*he colour of your skin is an issue. It was always an issue, is still an issue and will always be an issue. In fact let me go so far as to say, it was meant to be an issue.

Throughout history, skin colour has always been an issue and has played a major part in the unfolding of history. Colour, race . . . it is foolish to disregard their significance in the unfolding of history and in the changing fortunes of man. This truth is even more relevant to Black People hailing from the African continent and scattered in most nations of this world-this, for the most part, not by choice. It is important for the sake of the future of nations and the future of Black People in particular, to call the lie which has been spun almost into conventional wisdom in the so called global village-*"the colour of your skin does not matter"*. As always the naive, be they individuals, groupings or political leaders, are always taken advantage of by those to whom this lie is convenient.

So I come back to challenge you to be awakened to a simple truth:

You will be judged by the colour of your skin.

It is so significant that that great spiritual, social and political Black Prophet, the Rev. Martin Luther King Jr., put so much stock into the issue of judgement. As a messianic messenger fighting to lead Black People into redemption from centuries of oppression, slavery and exploitation by fellow humans of other skin colours, he came up with the truly memorable statement, "I have a dream that my four children will one day live in a nation where they will not be judged by the colour of their skin, but by the content of their character". Of course, the Dream, and I concur with *the whole Dream*, to me as a Black Person and to many noble hearted people of other colours, the Dream, *the whole Dream, is sacred.* Yet, as is essential with all sacred sayings and writings, it is necessary to look deeper in order to find abiding truth.

"Will be judged . . ." he said. The Almighty designed this life, this world, this existence in such a way that it would be a playing field in which individuals, groups, communities and even races would compete for space, stature and resources. Physical and psychological resources that is, not only in order to survive, but also to be fulfilled in making a dignified, albeit diversified contribution to mankind's unfolding progress in every field.

It is because of this that it is natural for human beings to size one another up, to judge. How you are judged in any arena determines at least the perception of what you deserve and what you are worth. A major part of human perception rightly or wrongly depends on what appears to the eye, what is seen. The colour of your skin is the first thing that appears concerning you. And it evokes judgments for better or for worse-much of the time judgement by stereotypical association with a group.

For this reason-that you will be judged by the colour of your skin-my thesis is that wisdom and experience dictate to the Black person that it is you the Black person who must dictate how you are judged by the colour of that skin. Of all judgements, it is self-judgement which is most critical, and the Black person has betrayed himself and his children by abrogating his right to be his own judge by the colour of his skin.

Throughout history, Black People have not only allowed other nations to pass judgement on them but have also succumbed to those judgements. It is clear that the Black person only grants himself personal approval when he attains standards dictated by people of other colours. When you take that position, you become a victim. Indeed what really matters at the end of the day may not so much be by what standard you are judged, but *who* passes that judgement.

It is evident that throughout history, nations have only become great when they have broken free and begun to judge themselves—to set their own standard. India only started on the path to greatness when Mahatma Ghandi taught Indians to reject the British standard and adopt an Indian one—this to the place of even burning clothing manufactured in Manchester and spinning, weaving and wearing Indian cloth with a pride that can only be born out of a positive self judgement. It may have taken some time, but the reason why great indigenous companies have risen from Indian soil and even bought up companies in Great Britain, the former colonial power, is this decision on the part of Indians to adopt self judgement and to set their own standard. The story is the same with the Chinese, the Japanese, the Arabs, and the Jews—the list goes on. There can be no greatness for those who dwell perpetually in the shadows of masters and big brothers.

Those who set up their own standard, who practise self-judgement, release themselves to make their rightful contribution to mankind in all fields. The fact that you find everything from Indian and Chinese foods to products in nations that formally regarded themselves as superior to these peoples is testimony to the fact that those who begin to judge themselves desirable begin to be competitive in the eyes of other peoples.

Dear Africa, dear Black People in Europe, United Kingdom, United States of America, and all the Americas, the Caribbean and all over this Global Village: hear me! It is time to wake up! Peoples of other nationalities and colours whom God in His wisdom put upon the face of this earth have through the generations taken up much more than their share of the resources of the earth and gone on to make far reaching contributions to the progress of mankind. It is not hard to associate certain products and achievements with the Peoples of the east and of the west-with the Reds and the Whites. I agree of course that many of these achievements and resources were unfairly acquired by victimising and plundering the Black People at their most vulnerable points in history. This was done through conquest, the slave trade, colonialism, neo-colonialism and many other forms of subterfuge in which especially the White People excelled and, in some cases, continue to excel.

But the time has come for us to shake off all this and answer the call of history and destiny. In 2010, and because of the soccer world cup being held in Africa, in South Africa, I heard again and again these prophetic words-prophetic in a way that reaches far beyond a mere game of soccer-being beamed by satellite television into every nation of the earth: *It's time for Africa! Ke nako!*—the clear convinced voice of the African woman proclaimed to the whole world.

Of course to many who happen to think that it is business as usual, these words simply meant that it is time for yet another safari in the playground of Africa where men and women of other colours come and enjoy the resources of a People who have not yet fathomed the value of what is their own. But discerning people, Black People and their allies of other colours, heard an immensely farther reaching and travailing cry in the voice of that queenly African woman. *Ke nako!*-she hailed, like Africa the Woman, declaring, "It's time for me to give birth!" She was not just saying that it's time for Africa to host soccer. She was saying, *"It is about time Africa, Black People, took their share of the earth's resources, achieved their quota and made their uniquely African contribution to this world."*

In that voice were compressed the cries and travails of Black Prophets, from Zephaniah and the Queen of Sheba of the Bible, to Booker T Washington with his Up from Slavery, to Harriet Tubman with her Underground Railroad smuggling Black people out of slavery, to Rosa Parks with her defiant ride on the segregated bus in the racist American South, to Marcus Garvey, to Malcolm X, to the Reverend Martin Luther King Junior with the Dream, to the Reverend Jesse Jackson, to African liberators like Kwame Nkrumah, Patrice Lumumba, Amilcar Cabral, Julius Nyerere, Leopold Senghor, Jomo Kenyatta, Kamuzu Banda, Kenneth Kaunda, Joshua Nkomo, Robert Mugabe, Seretse Khama, Eduardo Mondlane, Samora Machel, Queen Nzinga and Aghostino Neto of Angola, Sam Nujoma, Oliver Tambo, Bantu Steven Biko, Walter Sisulu, Nelson Mandela, Thabo Mbeki and many more whom I reluctantly fail to mention for lack of time and space.

The cry, Ke nako or, *It is about time!* as I put it, assumes a serious urgency because, through the seasons of Political Liberation spanning four hundred years from Slavery and Emancipation, to Colonialism and Political Liberation culminating in the liberation of South Africa from Apartheid in 1994, Black People began to realise their Dream, then tragically aborted it almost as soon as struggle yielded opportunity! The chief blunder was to abandon the powerful maxims of the early Black Prophets and Prophetesses of the African Dream who insisted that Black People set their own standards and become their own judges instead of aspiring to ape the standards of other Peoples.

It is amazing how the voices of Black Prophets like Malcolm X, Bantu Steven Biko, Patrice Lumumba, Marcus Garvey and any others who urged a stand for Blackness, have been silenced or reduced to token mention. This by Black governments and leaders who have surrendered to an anachronistic vision of leading their people to aspire for the approval and acceptance of People of other colours through adopting an absurd White-Blackness. Black political and other leaders do not seem to understand the far reaching damage which this step backwards is wreaking on present and future generations of Black People, in effect ensuring that Black People as individuals, communities and nations will stand little chance of future competitiveness among Peoples of other colours.

Have you noticed how religious, serious and jealous people of other colours are about their history, values, standards and prophets? White people for example will insist that even Black people learn their history, values, heroes and prophets. Almost every educated Black person, even a child, will know about Napoleon, Columbus, Queen Victoria, Abraham Lincoln, Cecil Rhodes, Paul Kruger, while Black heroes, even those whose priceless contributions and sacrifices are as recent as the twentieth century, are hastily dumped into inexplicable archives. In the rare instances where White people have allowed the names of

Black heroes to be mentioned, they have depicted them as defeated savages, while sanitizing villains of their own colour.

Why are Black people ashamed even of their own Liberation Struggles? Why are we hiding our history, culture and values from our children? Why does a Black person in Europe or America have a perception that African-ness is a primitive savagery from which he should distance himself? Why is the Black person hanging his head in shame and raising his children as a confused cocktail of alien values and cultures?

The truth is that when people have abandoned their God-given prerogative of self-determination, that is, to judge themselves and to set their own standards, they have set the stage for their own extinction and denouement by other Peoples. This today is the reality of the Black person in the global village.

African voices continue to speak to the generations of Africa

Oliver Tambo, 1917-1993. *Visionary Anti-Apartheid Leader, Co-founder of ANC Youth League and President of ANC*

Chapter 2

African Freedom Statue in Lusaka, Zambia

None but ourselves: The African Freedom Statue in Lusaka Zambia captures the message of self-reliance: that Black people should themselves break all chains of oppression, be they mental, psychological or economic.

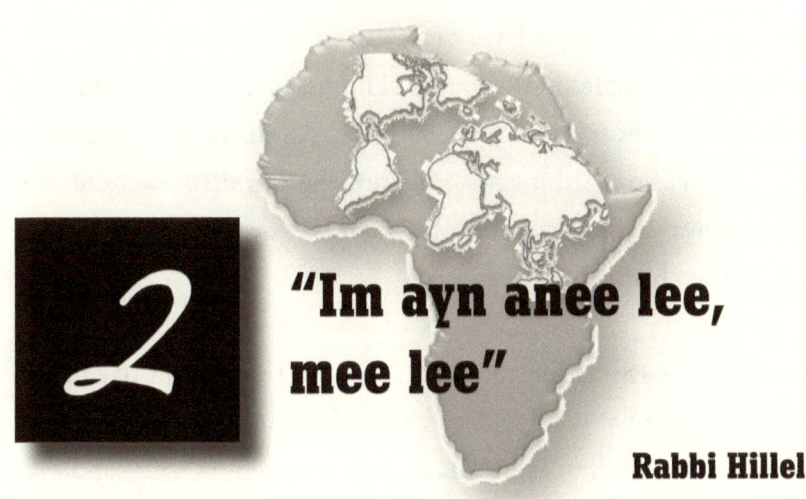

2 "Im ayn anee lee, mee lee"

Rabbi Hillel

Im ayn anee lee, mee lee.

Rabbi Hillel

Don't feel too bad if you can't make sense of the words above. They are Hebrew words approximated with our usual alphabet. They are the words of Rabbi Hillel who was one of the Jewish teachers in the days of Roman occupation and oppression and the Jewish struggle against it. *Im ayn anee lee, mee lee,* simply means *if I am not for myself, who is?.*

In other words

> *The first person who must believe in me is me.*
> *The first person who must affirm and support me is me.*
> *The first person who must stand for me is me.*
> *The first person who must fight for me is me.*

I believe the Black People, the African Nation worldwide, have priceless lessons to learn from the Jewish Nation, the Jewish People, worldwide. There is an uncanny similarity in the histories of these two nations which seems to me to be no coincidence. Both Peoples have experienced in uncanny ways unique brutalisation by other Peoples in the jungle of human competition for space, presence, resources and sheer primacy. Words like enslavement, discrimination, victimisation, oppression, subjugation, dispossession, displacement and genocide are common to these two Peoples in ways experienced by no other Peoples in the known history of mankind.

The journey of the Jewish nation through history to the present day makes intriguing and inspirational reading. Convinced from the very beginning of their Divine origin and destiny as well as of their uniqueness, value and self-worth, this through the voices of their founding fathers and Prophets—the Jews navigated perilous waters and have survived to make outstanding contributions to mankind in every field. Literature, Religion, Economy, Culture, Politics—all these fields are enriched by luminaries from this one Nation. Who would have imagined that Moses, Jesus Christ, Karl Marx, Albert Einstein, the Oppenheimers, Henry Kissinger, Golda Meier, Madeleine Albright and many others would all emerge singularly from a People who can only through the ages be described as a threatened species?

The Jews survived enslavement in Egypt, colonisation by the Romans, several Diasporas from Babylon to the post 70 A.D. dispersion which ended in 1948 with the birth of the State of Israel, economic plunder from Rome to Adolf Hitler, prejudice and genocide which climaxed in the holocaust—the slaughter of over six million Jews presided over by Adolf Hitler in the 1939 to 1945 Second World War and a present day existence in which they are surrounded by hostile Peoples. From it all, they emerged with a philosophy embodied in two words: **never again.** Simply put, this means, like Hillel and the other Prophets taught them, they will be for themselves and they will fight any and everything that seeks to destroy them as a People.

You may agree or disagree with the politics of this People, but one thing is clear—the Jews are an outstanding study of a People who have survived without other Peoples' permission.

Let us be clear about two principles which are two sides of the same coin. These are principles which the Black People, beginning with our Religious, Political and other Leaders, going on to every man, woman, boy and girl, must of critical necessity, adopt. First, *it is the God given duty of every People to survive the efforts of other Peoples, no matter how cunning or brutal, to destroy or to extinguish them.* Second, *it is the God assigned Mission of every People to fight for the survival of the essence of who they are, for only from this essence can they make their God—assigned contribution to Mankind.*

Put in another way, this is a world in which the Black People must wake up to the fact that they are a threatened species. Because of this, the Black People must a. *Survive Blackness* and b. *Cause Blackness, African-ness, with the essence of its God given riches for Mankind, to survive.*

There is no doubt that Blackness, African-ness, has always been under mortal threat and assault. History also clearly testifies that this assault by other Peoples is not coincidental, but rather planned and orchestrated.

Witness first the Slave Trade—a traumatic holocaust which Arabs and White People brought to Africa. With weapons superior to the Black People's bows and arrows, they captured mainly young Black men, women, boys and girls. In chains, they packed them in ships' holds like cargo to sail, cushioned by their own excrement and surrounded by the rotting corpses of fellow kinsmen waiting for disposal, to distant lands like the Americas. There they sold or auctioned them off to White People who would force them to labour in plantations and other vehicles of the masters' enrichment at no charge. Every time I visit that slave post on the West African coast and see the *'door of no return'* where Black people, snatched from their families, exited the dungeons to enter the slave ships, I suffer fresh bouts of horror and trauma. But I do it, lest I forget.

Witness the 1884 Berlin Conference in which a People united by the white colour of their skins, sat down around a table, and as brothers, cousins and nephews, held a workshop in which they discussed how they could divide portions of the African continent and People among themselves without fighting among themselves and killing anyone of their own colour. They sanitised and dignified this table where the strategy for the slaughter and dispossession of the Black People was planned over cups of tea, with the name, "The Berlin Conference". This culminated in the era of Colonialism in which Africa was divided, occupied, ruled and its resources plundered and exploited for and from Europe.

Witness the fact that the evil of colonialism was in our time dismantled, not voluntarily, but by sustained Liberation Struggles and wars in which many more Black people were slaughtered. Witness also the fact that the genocide of Black People through the Slave Trade and Colonialism far exceeded the genocide of the Jewish People both in numbers and in scope. The Black People were not only slaughtered physically, but were left in many cases with the eternal trauma of being bereaved of their identity, origins and culture. To date a White American, whether in Brazil or in the United States, can tell you the tribe and village in Europe where he hails from, while the African American has no idea where he came from, his tribe or even his name! This not by choice, but because the slave master forcibly erased African identity and nomenclature.

I believe every Black person should read or watch Alex Haley's *Roots*, and that it should be made a compulsory part of every Black child's education. Providentially, the only essence of African-ness which the White slave master could not destroy was the Black skin, and this Blackness should be treasured and used by African People as a rallying point for their unity.

Witness the fact that through the traumatic after effects of Slavery and Colonialism, most Black People in Africa and around the world are fighting hard to become little Englishmen or Frenchmen and that Black young people everywhere are a study of identity and cultural schizophrenia. Witness the fact that directly as a result of this traumatic history, most Black People suffer from an almost chronic case of industrial size inferiority complex among peoples of other colours, and if things continue as they are, will pass it on to their children. Witness the fact that in the larger picture, again because of these traumas, the vision of many Black governments and politicians is simply to please or be acceptable to the standards and judgements of White people and governments in particular.

I put it to you that Blackness, African-ness, has been and continues to be under siege and assault. Black people must not only survive this siege but must simultaneously fight it in order to make the life-giving essence of African-ness survive in the same ways the Jews and other nations have fought for the survival of their essence and existence.

I am sure you must be wondering how I think the colour of the Black skin is an issue in this assault. The primary target of the Peoples that dispossessed the Black People was of course space, resources and primacy. I watched a historical movie in which an English king was underlining to his chancellor in the British winter that the Empire must survive so that the English may have their sunshine around the world. Even predators like Cecil Rhodes came to Southern Africa for sunshine on medical advice. Gold, ivory, diamonds, land! The lure was irresistible. But in order to justify the enslavement, colonisation and dispossession of the Black People, a philosophy had to be created. This philosophy was that the Black Person, because of the colour of his skin, was not really human, but rather some kind of savage animal species. Writings, teachings and statements to this effect were propagated, until even in families, children were trained into this line of thinking. Some White Christian missionaries had a tough time challenging this thinking among the predator class.

This philosophy would make it right to dispossess or slaughter the Black People then have a good night's sleep after killing 'apes' even for sport. Colonialism or enslavement became a humanitarian work in which savages were trained and civilised. A favour was being done. And ideas like this die hard. I visited a European nation a few years ago, and while we were going up the elevator, a little White boy kept tugging his mother's dress and telling her something while he excitedly pointed at me and my Black companions. My Black interpreter laughed, and I couldn't help laughing too at the innocence of the child when I was told what he was saying. The little boy was saying to his mother, who no doubt had taught him, in private, this identity of the Black Person, "Mama, monkeys!" It's tragic, I know, but it still brings a chuckle to my throat whenever I think of it. Yet you can still see the evidence of this kind of upbringing when Black people are called apes at sporting events and when political philosophies like apartheid and segregation, still fresh in our memories, hold entire nations to ransom. But worst of all, it still results in economic and social dispossession through prejudice and discrimination.

I find it at this moment necessary to record a disclaimer. I do not recount the above history to whip up racial hate and conflict. This book is not about hate, just as all the accounts and commemorations of the Jewish holocaust are not about hate, but about the preservation of a people and their potential contribution to mankind. Blackness, African-ness is essential for all mankind in the same way the vegetation and its photosynthesis are necessary for human survival. It must be fought for, and I am grateful for people of all colours who have fought and continue to fight in good conscience to help the Black People survive Blackness and cause its essence to survive to benefit the world. In God's economy, it was the slave trading Pharaoh's daughter who preserved the Jews' liberator, Moses, from her father's death sentence.

We Black People will never forget William Wilberforce, who fought in the British Parliament for slavery to be abolished. We will never forget the Christian Missionaries who fought moral battles against their People to assert that Black People are equal and as human as other Peoples. We will not forget the White people who fell in our struggles and even White nations that supported our wars of liberation. We will not forget the protests and boycotts by White individuals and groups that benefitted our struggles. If we forgot, we would be denying one of the key characteristics of our Black essence.

But my Mission is to call all Black leaders and People again to the message so aptly enunciated by the Rabbi—*Im ayn anee lee, mee lee? If I am not for myself, who is?* You see, there are several things all Black People must realise if we are to survive the assault on Blackness, on African-ness, and to fight for the survival of the God given essence of our Blackness so that we can make our contribution to mankind. We must firstly recover our sense of value, dignity, beauty and Divine origins. Secondly, we must assert ourselves with a determination to take our fair portion of the space and resources of the earth. And thirdly, we must react radically to rid our minds of the effects of the assault against Blackness.

Chief of these effects is that those who fought us don't have to fight us anymore because we are fighting ourselves by despising our Blackness and allowing others to be our judges and heroes and aspiring to their standards. We must fight again to be African—to rediscover African-ness and to express it in our lives, families, children, youth, communities, churches and above all in the evolution of our young nations. We must then stand side by side with other peoples as Africans, not as a confused mass defeated by premature assimilation.

A critical step in this direction is to realise that *those who forget will be victims again.* It continues to puzzle me why our Black politicians, Governments and Religious and other leaders are working so hard to cooperate with the current weapon of those who destroyed us in the past. This weapon is that of sending Black People into a race to *forget things which are lethal for a People to forget.*

Our dispossessors first buried all the positive history of the Black People because they knew fully well that those who don't know where they are coming from will not know where they are going to. Black People and their children know only White history and heroes. Then they buried the entire record of the holocaust of Black People for four hundred years at the hand of White People. Black People, unlike the Jews, know nothing anymore about the Slave Trade, Colonialism, resources of which they were dispossessed and how.

They are keen to forget about their struggles and wars of liberation, preferring to teach their children about Napoleon, Abraham Lincoln and the battle of Waterloo. Their own liberators are not being taught to them as heroes, and an African youth admires United States Marines attacking Iraq rather than Umkonto We Sizwe, ZANLA, ZIPRA, MPLA, FRELIMO, SWAPO or MAU MAU armies fighting for the liberation of Black People. Names like Bantu Steven Biko, Malcolm X, Marcus Garvey, Kwame Nkrumah and others are forgotten as are ideals of Pan Africanism—simply because it is now supposed to be politically incorrect to express ideas of African-ness. We are the only People who need no identity while other nations remind us day and night of their ancient wars whether just or evil, and keep their heroes alive on our screens and publications!

This is the kind of social, cultural and political folly which will lead Africans, Black People back to political, cultural and economic slavery. Only this time it will be voluntary. If Black People are not for Black People, then who is?

African Voices continue to speak to the generations of Africa

Booker T. Washington, 1856-1915. Born in slavery, he attained freedom, educated himself and inspired Black people to rise above the damage of slavery, educate and develop themselves. His book, 'Up From Slavery' is an all-time classic.

Chapter 3

The African village is the cradle of the wholesome values of Black people. The dog is an icon of the village.

The Village Icon

*N**o one can make you feel inferior without your permission.*

Eleanor Roosevelt.

One of the seasons of my life which I will always remember with nostalgia is growing up as a boy in the African village. I wish every person and especially every Black child would have the opportunity at some stage of their lives to live in the African village. The round grass-thatched huts, cool in summer and warm in winter. The sweet aroma of fresh cow dung when the women have treated the floor. The warm fire place round which we would sit cross legged at night with the smoke stinging our eyes as mother, father, grandmother, grandfather, told us folk stories, rich with life lessons. The full starry or moon lit sky at night as a child went out in hurried trepidation to fetch wood for the fire. The meal which we shared gathered in a circle breaking pieces of mealie porridge and dipping in the same gravy bowl, waiting for the eldest child to exercise his birth right and pick the first piece of meat. The prayers mother prayed with us before bed time. The grass mat we would lie on under a shared blanket as we slept or listened in the darkness with awe for the gallop of the witch's hyena. The chilly early mornings as we went out at dawn to harness the cows for ploughing. The fresh smell of the soil as we turned it with the plough or tilled it with our hands. The harvest. The once or twice weekly bath in the river. The fist fights in the bush as we took care of the goats, sheep and cattle. Occasional meetings of the community. The special four mile walk to church and back on Sundays.

But for some reason, my most intriguing memory of the African Village is *the village dog*. The dog was the icon of the African village. He would usually be quite lean as the people were wont to give him good meals, and he would survive on porridge and water and the occasional scraps. This was not because of the villagers' sadism towards animals. The dog was kept lean for the sake of the hunt.

The dog though had a habit that fascinated me even as a child. He would be lying on the ground fast asleep in the afternoon sun. Then, with no prompting he would suddenly get up and walk alone straight in a certain direction, and disappear, sometimes for hours at a time. If you looked carefully at him when he came back, you would see tell—tale traces of blood on his mouth that betrayed the fact that his unsanctioned and unannounced journey had been to a unilateral hunt where he would feed himself with the catch. This interesting behaviour spawned in the minds of the village wise men the African saying; *fungira mumoyo rwendo rwembwa,* translated literally, "thinking in the heart the journey of a dog". This simply means the dog will go on certain journeys which you cannot control because, they are born in his own thoughts and desires.

Eleanor Roosevelt was the wife of a distinguished American President. She inspired many Black People in the oppressed and prejudiced societies of the United States of America when she came up with a profound statement, "No one can make you feel inferior without your permission". She was communicating a powerful truth akin to the wisdom of the village dog; *your desires, actions, dreams and achievements are determined only by how you choose to think—by your mind.* You don't have to feel inferior to anybody just because they think you should be. In the castle of your free mind you can choose to take the attitude of ancient Job, "What you know, I know, I am not inferior to you".

The most critical battle Black People everywhere have to fight and win in order to survive Blackness and to ensure the survival of the essence of Blackness, is the battle of the mind—your way of thinking. Bantu Steven Biko one of the greatest champions in the war for African-ness, which he aptly termed *Black Consciousness,* put it this way: *"The most powerful weapon in the hand of the oppressor is the mind of the oppressed".* In this short statement he summed up the core strategy of those who for ages have fought to annihilate Black People and the essence of their African-ness.

From the beginning the strategy of the White predator class was to shape the mind and thinking of the subjugated Black People into such a mode that they would always think in lowly and inferior ways about themselves. This was done first through traumatising acts of savagery such as enslavement and the humiliation of the constant slave master's whip on the bare back. Bob Marley captured it well when he sang:

> *Every time I hear the crack of a whip*
> *My blood runs cold*
> *I remember on the slave ship*
> *How they brutalised our souls*
> *Now they say that we are free*
> *Only to be trapped in poverty . . . .*

Segregation which ensured that the Black person could not eat, drink or even go to the toilet in the same good facilities as White people, nor live in the same areas throughout the seasons of slavery and colonialism, supplied a daily illustration of inferiority. The right way to address any White person was 'Master', even in the case of Black old men addressing little White boys. In the early days of colonialism Black people would even be required to carry White persons who happened to be passing through, on manual carriages on their shoulders. Even in church, seating was segregated.

Then came the education system with content specially designed for the subjugation of the Black person. It was called 'Native education'. I can't forget how as a child growing up in a country under British rule we would start each school day with a song we were trained to sing with British zeal: *"God save our gracious Queen! Long live our noble Queen, God save the Queen. Send her victorious, happy and glorious, long to reign over us! God save the Queen."* This was not a prayer for the Black African Queen of Sheba, but for the White Queen of England. Then came the classroom where from history to geography and most parts of the curriculum we were taught that all good and clever things come from White people and that Black people were inferior beings who had the privilege of being discovered by White people. You were so trained that you understood and agreed that the wars of White people in which they dispossessed your ancestors were heroic wars on the part of the White people who defeated the savage Black Africans. Then came a training that elevated all things white in your mind—white food, white dress, white habits and culture, and despised all things Black.

In higher education Black people were as far as possible barred from opportunities to become doctors, scientists, lawyers, economists, engineers or technical people, and most degrees for Black people were in such things as languages and religious studies.

The media was also used very effectively to put down Black people and to elevate whiteness. Any countries which happen to have fallen under the rule of Black people was stereotyped as being destroyed by the incompetence of the Black People. Apartheid and its Group Areas Act crowned it all with its uncompromising segregation against Black people.

All these tactics were very effective in conditioning the mind of the Black person into a chronic state of inferiority complex and inordinate admiration of all things white. This to the point where the Black person sees no value in another Black person because he looks like himself, yet bears a great sense of value and even empathy for White people.

Steve Biko was right. The design of the White predator was amazingly shrewd. He took time to mould the mind of the Black person to be his tool long after even events like political Liberation would have taken place. Today because of this mental damage White people don't have to harm Black people. Black people don't value anything that looks like themselves so they slaughter one another in acts of political victimization and violence, abuse, needless wars, afro-phobia and crime—while the predators look on in glee at the efficient working of the mind that has truly become the most efficient tool in the hand of the oppressor.

In this problem lie even the roots of bad governance and political misdirection on the part of some leaders of the Black People. Ancient wisdom teaches us that people suffer when a slave becomes a king. A Black ruler who abuses his people does so because he has no sense of their value, because they look like himself, and he, through the mental damage of slavery and colonialism, does not value himself.

All over the world, day by day, all you have to do to witness the effects of this chronic inferiority complex which continues to work through the Black man for his oppressor and against himself is, *be Black*. Be Black at the border post of an

African country and stand in the queue with a White person. The White person will be served with a smile and outstanding gestures of affirmation. When you the Black person stand before the immigration officer he or she becomes annoyed by your sheer appearance and in many cases takes you through a round of humiliating processes equalled in their unpleasantness only by experiences at border posts of some western countries. Be Black in a department store whose floor service people are Black and watch them give preferred service to a White customer who came in after you. Be Black at a traffic police check point manned by Black officers and watch them sail the White motorist in front of you through with smiles while waiting to read you the riot act. Be Black in a restaurant staffed by Black waiters and watch them display open preference to the White clients at the next table—the list is endless.

I only list the above examples for their simplicity. The tragedy is that Black people display the same knack for victimising their own colour in critical areas such as awarding good contracts. In such an area that has far reaching effects on the economies of Black people the conventional wisdom continues to be, *White is better.*

When Steve Biko asserted that the most powerful weapon in the hands of the oppressor is the mind of the oppressed, He clearly defined the arena in which all leaders and people who desire to restore Black people to their rightful and competitive place among other peoples should fight the battle-*the arena of the mind.* Black parents, Black governments and political leaders, Black education departments, schools and colleges, Black media such as radio, television and newspapers, should invest heavily and overwhelmingly in the mission of uncompromisingly and persistently renewing the minds of Black people with a special emphasis on children and youth. This renewal must begin with clearly showing the Black person the kind of damage which was historically perpetrated on his mind by People of other colours. The first step to healing a malady is to define it and understand its origins and causes. You cannot fight an enemy you cannot understand.

This is why Black people should be alarmed at the conspiracy to silence everyone on the subject of the wrongs that were done to the Black people throughout history. At the same time the world is being continually reminded of the wrongs that were done to Peoples of other colours, for example the Jews in the holocaust. We must not seek an impossible charity. It is Black people themselves who must trumpet the wrongs that were done to them to every generation, and inculcate in every Black person the vision of *never again*.

I have often heard the argument that the young generation of Black people who did not experience the slave trade and colonialism are free of inferiority, and should therefore not be defiled with accounts of the African Holocaust. Nothing could be further from the truth. The fact is, just as children and youths of other colours inherit the confidence and wealth advantage of their progenitors, and in many cases their prejudices, Black children and youths inherit the inferiority complex, poverty rooted in historic disadvantage and the self-hate of their progenitors. Their further disadvantage is that as they step out of the ghettos and slums and even suburbia affected by "White flight"—they cannot explain why they feel inferior and despise all things Black. This is a direct result of being kept in the dark by their elders concerning the Black holocaust. The inferiority complex of the Black young person as he rubs shoulders in a disadvantaged assimilation with young people of other colours is all the more devastating and dismaying because he has no idea why he feels and acts inferior. He cannot understand for example why he aspires to dress, eat, live and behave like a White European while his Indian, Chinese, Jewish, Arabic and other peers reflect identities and tastes distinctive to their respective Peoples.

Secondly Black leaders, governments, education departments and parents must invest in teaching Black People their origins, history, culture, language and identity. Any heroes in their history must be brought to their attention. In many cases, particularly in the case of Black people in the Diaspora occasioned for example by the slave trade, renewed programs must be mooted to inspire and facilitate all Black persons to identify their roots—that is, where they originated in Africa before being forcibly and violently uprooted by White slave traders, their tribes and languages as well. Modern genetic breakthroughs are making it more and more feasible to decipher the X in Malcolm X's name. One outstanding movement that will surely be a boon to all Black People is when African Americans for example utilize the advantages they have gained by being in America to channel different forms of development to areas of Africa which they will be inspired to identify with having recognized them as their original homes. This will not be foreign aid, but the home coming of African sons from the hunt, and African daughters from collecting fruits in the field.

Many Black People are these days being driven into a voluntary Diaspora into the Western world by economic conditions and opportunities. One watches with dismay as these people who grew up with wholesome personalities because their parents in Africa taught them their identity, language and culture, rob their own children of these vital things through sheer negligence and in some cases a foolishness born of an inferiority complex that makes them think that their children will find fulfilment in becoming, for example, as English as possible. One family told me that their Black child in a White school in Australia came home from school in tears one day, and appraised her mother tearfully of the tragic discovery she had made that day; "Mommy, I am not White!" Well the Biblical adage was "Can an Ethiopian (African) change his skin? The parents received a rude awakening that their child had suffered psychological damage directly as a result of their not teaching her at home the uniqueness, dignity and worth of her Black skin and heritage. Only in this way can Black children and youths stand shoulder to shoulder with their peers of other colours without any sense of inferiority and thus make their own unique Black contribution to mankind. It will require effort, but these Black children in the Diaspora must be taught their origins, identity, languages and cultural values and must be shown that these are equal to any other in the world.

A social worker in the United States of America once made me aware of a shocking statistic. He told me that African Americans make up less than a fifth of the population of the United States, but account for over half of the inmates in American prisons. He told me that the reason for this is a high level of crime among Black youth. The crime in turn is a result of a smouldering anger in the psyche of many young Black males. They are frustrated by their imposed ignorance of their identity in a nation dominated by a predominantly well off White male. While aspiring to be like this White male the reality of their colour and disadvantaged history haunts them and they vent this frustration and anger through violent crime. Contrary to what many Black people think, when a Black person is taught the true dignity of his colour, it heals his psyche and puts him at advantage in the competition with other Peoples. This is why a concerted effort must be made to teach all Black People their roots and dignity and value.

Next, the Black person needs to be taught and trained against any sense of entitlement and dependence, especially on other Peoples. One of the most debilitating results of the inferiority complex bequeathed upon the Black person is a sense that he has nothing to offer and must only receive help and ideas and things that come from other Peoples. When a People become aware of their true self-worth, their immediate response is, *what can we create, what can we give and what can we contribute to mankind?* The immediate response to needs should be *how can we solve this problem ourselves*, not other peoples must come and rescue us. Black People's dependency syndrome is born out of the powerlessness that was forced on them through slavery and colonialism. Even churches and other religions came to Black People with hand outs instead of arming them psychologically to have confidence restored in their minds that they can create their own solutions and help themselves in all situations. The man who gives you a fish impoverishes you. The man who teaches you to fish empowers you.

One Western leader inspired his people by telling them 'Ask not what your country can do for you, but rather what you can do for your country'. Many Black countries are paralysed by a national culture of a people who expect everything to be delivered to them by the government. Communities which could organize themselves easily to develop neighbourhoods for example by digging a simple drainage canal, will watch their children playing in the sewage effluent until the government one day comes to dig the trench.

Train Black young People, starting with little children in the home with charity piggy banks, to make donations to help other suffering peoples around the world. Governments must require Black young people to do national service in the form of time given for community help programs. Self-reliance as well as being of benefit to others are concepts that must be taught heavily in order to combat dependency syndrome.

Governments of Black ruled nations must, as a matter of urgency, direct their Education Departments to completely overhaul their Education and Training syllabuses from Kindergarten to Higher Education. The predator class which purpose—designed colonial and other education systems for Black People were very diligent in ensuring that the education would subjugate the Black person's mind in far reaching ways. It is therefore alarming that in most emerging Black Nations, only cosmetic changes, if any, have been made to syllabuses. It is a tragedy of monumental proportions that a graduate of a High School in a Black nation still knows more about Napoleon and Vasco da Gama than he does about King Shaka and Kwame Nkrumah.

Powerful think tanks must be convened to redesign the materials that schools teach, with the aim of recovering all that has been hidden or distorted concerning Black People, and of restoring the dignity and self-worth of Black People by telling them the simple truth about their history and heritage. I am persuaded that African culture contains the richest deposits of what should be taught in sociology, psychology and other related disciplines. There is no social system more mentally, materially, morally and emotionally supportive of the human person than the African extended family system and the humane, inclusive and compassionate social philosophy of *ubuntu.* Black intellectuals and educators must draw from these deep wells of African-ness and enrich the whole world with social models that are a clear answer to the disintegration, cynicism and moral decay we see in the societies of the so called developed world.

I really should spend the rest of the day talking about that multi faced, all powerful mega vehicle known as the Media. The Media—entertainment, television, radio, newspapers, publications—have for ages been used as *weapons of mass deception,* as one discerning African politician put it, to the mental disadvantaging of the Black person. Images, from newscasts to entertainment continue to be used to enhance inferiority into the minds of Black People. Political editorialising for example will melodramatise the mistakes of an African President while sanctifying massacres initiated by leaders of powerful White nations. The tragedy lies not so much in the unfairness as it does in the fact that Black People themselves end up accepting this judgement. As a result, they harbour an inordinate despising of their own leaders while carrying an irrelevant and ill placed admiration of even blood—thirsty leaders of far away Peoples.

Black Nations must take a serious view to the overhauling of the content and editorial leanings of their media. The media has the frightening ability to daily, hourly and even minute by minute, shape the minds of people in any nation. Leaders and professionals who want to work for the renewing of the minds of Black People must with urgency set out to change the content of the media to which their People are exposed.

A delicate balance must be struck in emerging Black nations between the concept of legitimate freedom of speech and protection of new national values from financially powerful media houses owned, run or serviced predominantly by former oppressors who still hold on to their former values or those of former colonial masters. In many cases the editorial lines of these media houses hold no African national interest in their values, but are brazenly determined by whatever are the current Western, especially right wing, editorial lines. Cartoons of Black leaders are drawn up, not for wholesome political satire, but for a deliberate and sustained ridiculing of African leaders designed to caricature them as inferior clowns unfit to govern countries. All this is hypocritically passed on as freedom of speech.

To one and all let me say: the wars and struggles for Liberation of Black People did not bring liberation. They brought the opportunity to begin to set our People free. The most important frontier in the war to set Black People free is the frontier of the mind. This war must be waged by all Black People and their leaders—whether political, religious, social, economic or intellectual—with an even greater shrewdness, tenacity, ferocity and determination than that employed by the predators who enslaved the minds of Black People.

It is not international aid packages which shall change the disadvantaged face of Africa and Black People everywhere. The key lies in changing the way of thinking in the minds of Black People everywhere. This is where the battle should be fought, and every Black man, woman and child needs to enlist as a warrior in this battle. Easily the most powerful statement in the Bible reads, *". . . you shall know the truth and the truth shall set you free."*

And if that is too deep for you, just learn from the African village dog. *It's time for Black People to go on a journey of their own thinking.* It begins with a renewed mind.

African voices continue to speak to the generations of Africa

Léopold Sédar Senghor, 1906-2001. African poet and intellectual and first President of Senegal. He was a visionary champion of Black dignity who co-founded the movement, 'Negritude' (Blackness), "There is no denying that negritude is a fact, a culture; it is the whole of economic and political, intellectual and moral, artistic and social values of not only the peoples of Africa but also of the black minorities of America, and indeed of Asia and Oceania."

Ancient Africa—Pioneers Of Progress

The Great Zimbabwe
(From which modern Zimbabwe derives its name)

As early as the fifteenth century, African people had built up kingdoms with sophisticated social, political, cultural, economic and architectural infrastructures.

There are at least 600 ruins of smaller stone built cities spread in the Southern African region—Zimbabwe, Mozambique and South Africa. Great Zimbabwe housed 80 000 people at its peak.

Ancient Southern Africans mined gold on an epic scale. One modern writer says: "The estimated amount of gold ore mined from the entire region by the ancients was staggering, exceeding 43 million tons"

Africa Fact

Africa is considered by many scientists to be the origin of mankind. The Cradle of Mankind first named by UNESCO in 1999 is in South Africa where fossil remains were found suggesting that the first habitat of Human beings was the African continent. Africa is indeed the Mother of all nations."

Ancient Africa—Pioneers Of Progress

Africans were the first to engage in mining.
In 1964 a hematite mine dating back 43,200 years was found in Swaziland, together with 300,000 artefacts and thousands of stone mining tools.

Africans pioneered basic arithmetic.
The Ishango bone dating back 25,000 years that was found in Zaïre (now Congo) has notches in formations that show doubling, addition, subtraction and prime numbers

Africans cultivated crops 12,000 years ago in West Africa. West Africa had flourishing cities dating back to 1000BC. Tools used by these ancients were also recovered.

Ethiopia minted its own coins over 1,500 years ago.

African voices continue to speak to the generations of Africa

Shaka kaSenzangakhona (Zulu), c1787-1828.
Founder of the Zulu Nation who united African tribes through a social and military revolution.

African Holocaust—Slavery

Black People, raided and abducted from their homes in Africa by weapon-wielding White slave traders were yoked and chained to one another and force marched to slave ships for the journey to exile and slavery.

The savagery of the slave trade resulted in the death of over twenty-two million Black people—by far the biggest holocaust and genocide in the history of mankind.

Africa Fact

Africa has 54 countries. South Sudan is Africa's newest country officially born on July 9, 2011. Africa is home to 15% of the world's population.

African Holocaust

A slave chained to a heavy beam awaiting shipment as cargo to Europe or America.

It was common for thousands to spend months packed in horrendous conditions in dungeons like this one as they awaited ships' arrival. Slave traders abused, raped, whipped or murdered their captives at will.

African voices continue to speak to the generations of Africa

Albertina Sisulu, 1918-2011.
Inspirational Anti-Apartheid activist who was embraced as a Mother of the South African nation.

African Holocaust

THE DOOR OF NO RETURN
Once the slave boats arrived, the slaves were herded through the "Door of No Return" and packed like cargo in ships in chains in the darkness below decks with no sanitary facilities for the long voyage to the slave auctions.

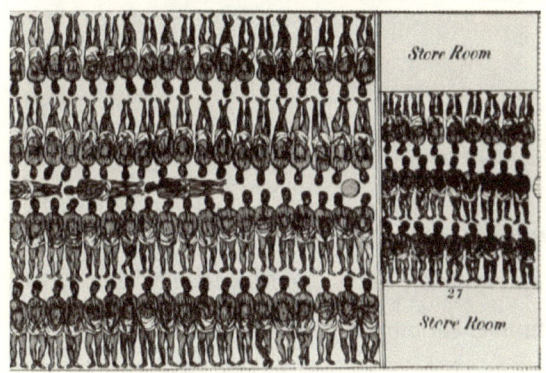

Slaves were chained and packed shelf-style below decks with no light or sanitary facilities.

Africa Fact

Africa has the world's largest solar energy capabilities due to the proximity of most of its land mass to the Equator. Most of Africa has at least 325 days of strong sunlight in the year, making massive renewable energy projects possible. Africa can light up every dark corner and all her industry with renewable energy.

African Holocaust

Sick, condemned or dead slaves were simply thrown overboard during the voyage.

Once the slaves arrived they were auctioned like property to the highest bidder, then taken to plantations to labour at the White master's pleasure.

African voices continue to speak to the generations of Africa

Sengbe Pieh, c1813-1879
A son of a Sierra Leonian Chief captured into slavery who led a revolt on the slave ship Amistad. This action had far reaching consequences leading to the abolition of slavery.

African Holocaust

It was common for the slave to be branded by the owner with a smouldering iron, just like a horse. Savage instruments were used to torture or restrain slaves. Slave babies were forcibly separated from their mothers.

Africa Fact

Africa has tremendous potential in arable land use. A FAO study estimates that if the potential is realised Africa's arable land use will increase from 150 to 700% and even more in countries with irrigation. If Africa does not cede her land to rich countries in unscrupulous deals that are reportedly on the rise, she can one day feed the world.

African Holocaust

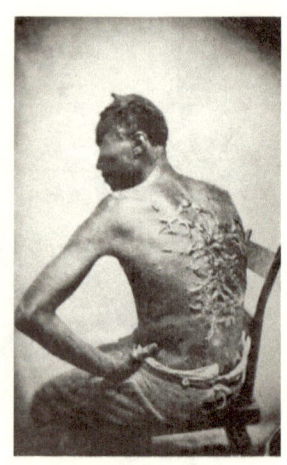

The scars of the continual slave master's whip. The brutality of the slave trade continued with the torture and massacres of colonialism.

African voices continue to speak to the generations of Africa

Modibo Keita, 1915-1977
A passionate Pan Africanist and the First President of Mali.

African Holocaust

The motive behind the African Holocaust through the slave trade was self enrichment through the free labour of Black people. The present day economic advantage of White People over Black People has its foundations in slavery and colonialism Here slaves toil in the cottonfields.

 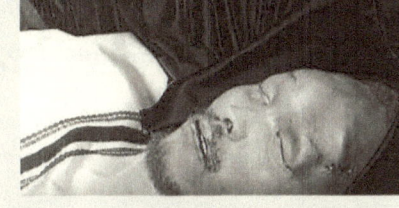

Steve Biko In Life   Steve Biko In Death

The Savagery Of White Racism Against Liberators Of Black People
Steve Biko was killed by Apartheid police who claimed he had starved himself.

The African Holocaust continued during the Liberation Struggles with the torture, assassination and killings of liberation leaders and activists, including children. The African Holocaust begs a resolution from leaders of Black people, "NEVER AGAIN".

Africa Fact

Africa is known for breathtaking natural beauty, vast spaces, endless deserts, raw wilderness, tropical rain forests, rugged mountains, fertile grasslands, glorious sunsets, thundering water bodies and diverse cultures. A large portion of the World's heritage is deposited in Africa—oldest rocks, massive wildlife, endangered fauna and flora, the oldest desert and rocks.

African Holocaust

One of the fitting Monuments to the thousands of gallant African freedom fighters who liberated African nations from colonialism through protracted and bloody wars in extremely hard conditions.

Urgent initiatives need to be launched portraying these exceptional warriors as heroes in the eyes of all Black people and of the youth in particular.

We are our own Liberators

African voices continue to speak to the generations of Africa

Alex Haley, 1921-1992
American author whose famous work ROOTS inspired Black People to seek and embrace their identity.

Chapter 4

True Religion must nurture the African Dream . A Church Service being enriched by traditional African Worship and Dance.

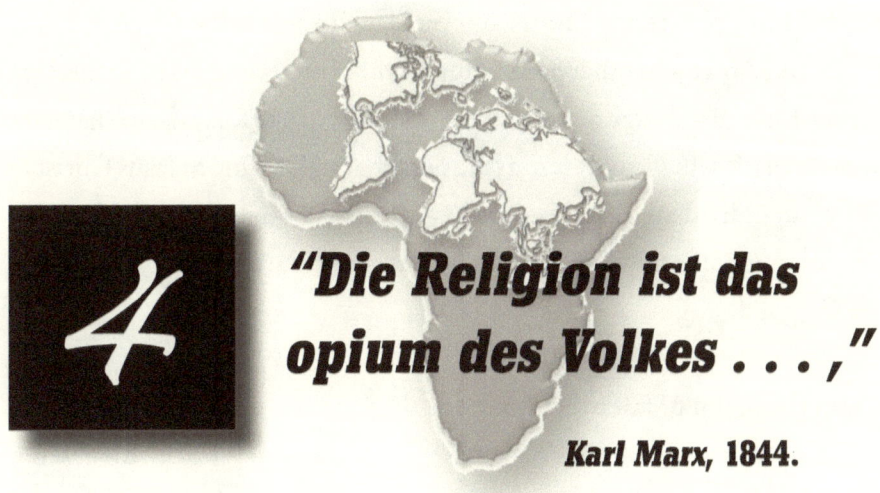

"Die Religion ist das opium des Volkes . . . ,"

Karl Marx, 1844.

D*ie Religion ist das Opium des Volkes.*

Karl Marx, 1844.

I am sure you are familiar with the name Karl Marx, the German Jewish socio-political thinker and his famous statement quoted above which simply means, *Religion is the opium of the masses.* Although he wrote this statement in 1844, in the heat of the Black People's Holocaust, I am unsure whether the plight of Black People was on his mind. Nonetheless, truth tends to have universal impact, and many of this man's ideas were adopted by leaders who fought for the freedom of Black People.

There is no doubt that African People—Black People all over the world have embraced Religion, and largely harnessed it for good even in times when societies in Europe tend to call themselves post-Christian. I am convinced that belief in God as Creator, Father, Law-Giver, Redeemer and final Judge ennobles all individuals and societies who choose to subscribe to it. Likewise absence of faith in God tends to debase human nature and bring out the worst in it.

One of the most progressive forces among Black People is the Church. In my travels all over Africa and other parts of the world, I have seen how by embracing the simple Biblical message of the redemption and change for good in character and quality of life which comes from the personal welcoming of Jesus Christ in the life of an individual, Black People have realised both their individual and collective potential as powerful congregations have been organised, mobilising people for good.

It is from the realm of faith that liberators like the Reverend Martin Luther King Junior and others have risen up. Most leaders of African Liberation will vouch to the fact that Churches worldwide played a powerful and supportive role in the struggles for the Liberation of African Peoples. Black People everywhere repose tremendous confidence in Religion in general, and in the institution known as the Church in particular. From the days of the Slave Trade, through Colonialism to the struggles of the present day, Black People have always looked to the Church as a City of Refuge. And so they should.

However, this situation places tremendous responsibility on all Religion, and on Churches, Church Leaders and members, teachers and Theologians in particular, to revisit the teaching and practice of the Church with a view to ensuring that it plays its proper role in empowering Black People to survive the onslaught against Blackness, and to enhance African-ness and its God intended contribution to all mankind. This is because historically and potentially, Religion and the Church have been used by the predator class as one of the most devastating weapons against Black People. Even a bizarre doctrine like Apartheid claimed Biblical justification.

It is for this reason that we need to take a closer look at the words of Karl Marx. His critique of Religion went as follows:

Religion is the sigh of the oppressed creature, the heart of a heartless world, and the soul of soulless conditions.

It is the opium of the people. The abolition of Religion as the illusory happiness of the people is the demand for their real happiness.

Criticism of Religion is therefore, in embryo, the criticism of that vale of tears of which Religion is the halo.

The paradoxical nature of Marx's statement has continued to be a subject of argument among scholars. On the one part he appears to portray the Church as the powerful force that must provide heart, soul and happiness to mankind. On the other hand he turns around and calls it a deceptive drug. I believe that Marx, as a human being like all of us, in need of a heart and soul was actually decrying the Church for not taking its proper role in bringing answers based on reality to the hearts, souls and social, economic and political lives of oppressed people. This message is relevant to Religion, to the churches today as they interact with the Black People who have so passionately reposed their trust in religion.

Hardly four years after Marx's critique, Charles Kingsley, a Canon of the Church of England, challenged Religion with the following statement: *We have used the Bible as if it were a mere special constable's book, an opium dose for keeping beasts of burden patient while they were being overloaded, a mere book to keep the poor in order . . . .*

In this indeed lies the continuing misdirection of the churches. I do subscribe to the necessity of teaching personal piety and spirituality—but this is only part of the God-given Mission of the Church. It is Religion, the Churches, that should be at the front line of teaching the Black Person his true God given worth, dignity and identity. It is also the Church which should clearly show the Black Person the damage that has been done to his psyche throughout history by Peoples of other colours, and show him how to be redeemed from his case of industrial size inferiority complex. Any Church which does not fulfil this ministry has failed Black People and even God Himself, because God is the greatest investor in the Black People.

It is common cause that much of what is being taught and practised in Black People's Churches, in African Churches, is simply an imitation of right wing American Evangelical preachers with their focus on limited issues of spirituality and blessing. These teachings offer the Black Person absolutely nothing with which to overcome the far reaching disadvantages historically forced upon his life. In fact many Black churches reinforce the damage and inferiority complex fostered on Black People by White People—by being a training ground for Whiteness—that misguided religious process in which the Black Person is taught that the more White he behaves and models his life and worship, the more spiritual or Godly he is. In these churches you find nothing exalting African-ness or Blackness—not the music, not the worship, not the liturgy, not the teaching.

In addition, the Christian churches have done serious harm to their mission by emphasizing a religion that focuses only on the individual. Clearly, the God of the Bible seeks to be the God of a People—the God of Nations—of which He is the purposeful Creator. The Bible goes to great lengths to chronicle His purposeful interaction with the Nation of Israel. While the Christian Church emphasizes individual redemption, Biblical Redemption in the Exodus was first of all a National Redemption meant to be a model of God's dealing with all Nations. The Egyptians had for four hundred years frustrated God's purpose for the contribution of the Hebrew Nation to mankind by enslaving them. God then sent Moses to lead the Hebrews into the Passover—a series of ceremonial observances in which they killed lambs, put their blood on door posts and roasted and ate together with bitter herbs the meat of the lambs, expecting to be given passage out of Egypt and slavery through Divine intervention that same night. God's judgement would simultaneously be visited on the Egyptians as their first born sons would die mysteriously and their pursuing army would be drowned in the Red Sea.

This National Redemption in which Hebrew leaders, Moses, then Joshua were enjoined to lead the Hebrews to their own land where their identity, dignity, self-determination and economy would be re-established through sustained teaching, training and battle, is theologically agreed by Christian teaching to be the basis of the salvation which Christ the Lamb of God brings to the world. The strange thing is that churches have totally ignored the fact that this Redemption is first and foremost the Redemption of a nation so that it may repossess its God given heritage in every dimension in order to fulfil God's purpose among mankind.

Churches should therefore teach a doctrine of **African Redemption**. This doctrine should clearly show Black people that the sacrifice of Christ was also for their Redemption from the enslavement and colonialism through which people of other nations brought a damage to their minds that was meant to frustrate their God assigned contribution to mankind. African Liberation, after four hundred years of subjugation strangely akin to the Hebrews' four hundred years of slavery, is definitely a result of Divine Redemption. The Christian church should therefore emphasise on teaching the Black person how to be set free from the damage which was done to him through subjugation so that he may be empowered to fulfil his God given purpose among the nations.

It is the Church which should affirm Black People's Liberation struggles by showing them clearly that their leaders in Liberation are fulfilling the same

Divine role that Moses fulfilled. It is also the Church which must affirm the role of the leaders of African Liberation, and underline to them their Divine obligation to continue the struggle, as Moses and Joshua did. This would be done by renewing and retraining the minds of Black People, and ingraining in them the culture of self-dependence and of fighting for the ownership of their and the world's resources.

Indeed, the Church must sanctify the struggles and wars of Liberation of the Black People for the just Pilgrimages which they are. I don't know whether you have noticed how diligently White People ennoble their wars and struggles, even ancient ones, through religious services and commemorations. It is the opposite with Black People. A Freedom Fighter in one of Southern Africa's Liberation Struggles recently remonstrated with me on how the negative attitude of contemporary preachers in Black Christian Churches towards Black Freedom Fighters and the struggles they fought in, has traumatised some Freedom Fighters into feelings of guilt and shame concerning these just and legitimate struggles. This is against a backdrop where young Black people have been conditioned to admire the fighters of any White war they know about.

Time has come for Black Religious leaders to do the overdue diligence of redeeming the wars, struggles and holocausts of Black People from the premature archives to which they have been confined, and conducting relevant religious services and commemorations of them. A worldwide service, for example, of Thanksgiving for Emancipation of Black People from slavery and Colonialism should be held in all churches, and particularly in Black Churches. May 25 is Africa Day. At the forefront of celebrating this day adopted to commemorate freedom of African nations and to inspire African Unity, should be Thanksgiving Services in all Churches, acknowledging the Divine roots of African Freedom.

There is a frightening phenomenon in modern Christianity in which Black People will flock to White churches and leaders whilst no matter how gifted a Black Preacher is, he will only be patronised by multitudes of his own colour. I believe with all my heart that churches should be a beacon shining forth the light of integration and synergy of the races. Yet it is hard to run away from the fact that the reason why it is only the Black Christians who seek the Ministries of White Christians is that Black Christians suffer from the very same inferiority complex, self-hate and inordinate admiration of White People which plagues Black People in other arenas of life. Nor can we close our eyes to the fact that the reason White Christians do not seek the leadership of Black Christians is, at best, that they have confidence in themselves—in their own colour, and at worst that they still suffer from the same ungodly superiority complex that spawned enslavement of Black People.

We should wake up to the fact that it is in Religion that many stereotypes that stigmatised Blackness and exalted Whiteness were fabricated. Chief of these was, God is White and the Devil is Black. For this reason, many sectors of Religion regarded the struggles of Black People for equality and freedom as either evil or as a worldly pursuit in which people of true faith should not involve themselves. This has remained the Achilles' heel of churches that represent modern Christian revival.

The fact that even powerful Christian Broadcasting networks ignore issues of social justice, colour and the traumas of Black People while millions of their Black adherents need serious ministry in this area—is making faith irrelevant or hypocritical in the eyes of many Black People.

Hypocritical, because the Bible is not silent on issues of social injustice, racism and even colour bar. In the Book of Exodus for example, God curses Moses's sister, Miriam with leprosy for mocking Moses because he married a Black woman. Jesus himself goes out of his way to defy Jewish racism by interacting with a Samaritan woman and affirming her before prejudiced Jewish men. You would think pulpits and the airwaves would reverberate with preaching from texts of this nature, affirming Blackness against racism. But alas, a conspiratorial silence! What kind of God keeps silence on issues such as these which are a heavy yoke on the neck of millions of His Creatures? Is this not the proverbial petty holiness that strains a gnat and swallows a camel? Modern Evangelical Christianity should digest the sobering thought that Black People are not blind as to which Religions are seeking to be relevant to their deepest need.

Ultimately, it is the Black Religious leader, Minister, teacher, theologian, church person who must wake up to the fact that the church is the most important spring of hope for a Black restoration and Renaissance. It is here where masses of Black People flock voluntarily once, twice even thrice weekly looking for teaching, healing, ministry and guidance. It is here that Black People must hear a clear voice affirming their God purposed Blackness and the contribution God wants it to make among the nations. It is here that Black People must hear the voices that chronicle their holocausts and traumas clearly and point to the path of redemption and healing from the effects of enslavement. It is here again that Black People must be taught like Job of old to say to Peoples of other colours to whom they have felt inferior, "What you know, I know; I am not inferior to you." It is here that they must be taught self reliance, responsibility and creativity and embrace a mission to take the Promised Land.

It is here that Black children must be taught the beauty of their colour and the Divine origins and greatness of their progenitors such as Cush, Keturah the Black wife of Abraham, Jethro the Black priest, the Black wife of Moses, the great African Queen of Sheba who charmed King Solomon, the great African Prophet, Zephaniah who saw Black People from beyond the rivers of Ethiopia come to worship God, Simon the African who carried the cross of Jesus, and

Simeon Niger and other Africans who ordained Paul the great missionary. It is in the church that a deliberate emphasis on the expression of Black things, African things, must be mooted—so that we hear African rhythms, dance, music and lyrics in the worship, to the accompaniment of African instruments of music—the eternal drum, rattles, marimba and trumpets of rams' horns. It is here that the colours of African dress must bloom, and church luncheons and dinners where indigenous nutritious African dishes are rediscovered and re-dignified. It is here where Diaspora Africans must organise classes where their children learn their mother tongues, history and culture.

As African political leaders have fought to liberate Black People and to build the African Nation, the Black preacher has persistently prophesied to them to be spiritually correct in their politics, and rightly so. But as we have called upon politics and governance of Black People to be spiritually correct, it is even more important that the Preacher and the Church be *politically correct.*

Religion which does not identify with the needs and aspirations of its people provides an illusory happiness—*that Religion is the opium of the masses.*

African voices continue to speak to the generations of Africa

Marcus Garvey, 1887-1940.
Jamaican staunch proponent of Pan Africanism, Nationalism and economic freedom.

Chapter 5

Plenary meeting of African Union Heads of States. The most important and strategic frontier for the progress of Black people is the battle for African Unity.

5 The Ultimate Weapon

*B*ehold the people is one, and they all have one language; and this they begin to do: and now nothing will be restrained from them, which they have imagined to do.

The Almighty

*I*n all Religion, it is generally agreed that God is the all—powerful Creator whom mere humans, like you and me, can never begin to rival in thought, word or deed. This is why the story surrounding the above quote of words attributed to God Himself, has puzzled ordinary believers and religious scholars alike.

Apparently, when His mortal creatures, endowed with one language, decided in unity of purpose to build the Tower Babel—an edifice which would reach heaven, God Almighty and His heavenly council sensed the possibility that, in this mode, men would achieve the powers of unlimited accomplishment which would rival even the divine agenda. The solution to this unprecedented problem would be to divide their languages, and thus defeat their undesirable unity of purpose—we presume mischievous purpose.

Herein lies one of the most important, indeed critical, frontiers of the war to restore Black people and African-ness to the place where Black People worldwide can retrieve their heritage and competiveness, and make their unique contribution to all mankind. This critical frontier is perhaps the most important battle of all which Black People must fight—the war for African Unity, that is, the unity of Black People both on the continent of Africa and worldwide. Indeed, the divine tactic stated above is fail proof. The best strategy for destroying a people's potential is to rob them of their unity of purpose by dividing them.

Both during the days of subjugation, and when the Black People began to shake off the shackles of slavery and colonialism, a powerful and devastating weapon was fashioned against them by their former dominators—*the weapon of divide and rule*. This of course was a well-chosen weapon, considering its origins in divine strategy against human mischief. Only, in this case it would be used as a predator's strategy against Black Peoples' right and legitimate struggles to rebuild their shattered nationhood, identity, dignity, sense of self-worth and competitiveness among nations.

The state of division and failure to work together purposefully among Black People at various levels is all too obvious. What is not clear to many is that the pervasiveness of these divisions is too systematic to have been spontaneous. It was orchestrated by oppressors as a weapon they knew would sustain their stranglehold on Black People long after their political liberation would have been accomplished.

When you study the history of nations, power, wealth and competitiveness have always been a result of the ability to come together, dwell, work and trade together in unity of purpose. The word *united* in most cases preceded the names and description of nations and peoples who attained meaningful greatness and competitiveness—United States of America, Union of Soviet Socialist Republics, European Union, and so forth—unity and working together always precedes greatness.

Consider, if you can the nature of Black People's divisions. First of all the borders of African 'nations' are bizarre and unnatural legacies of colonialism which in all cases cut unceremoniously through the lands of great African peoples, dividing them so that parts of the same people would be fractured into different colonial 'nationalities'. Today Africans passionately preserve borders which were created not by them, but by those who subjugated them. No wonder the Berlin Conference of 1884 is historically titled *The Partition of Africa*. To partition simply means to divide and cut into small pieces. This is what White nations in Europe deliberately did to Africa

Often within those 'nations', the White people ensured future enduring division of Black People by patronising one tribe against another. The Belgians, for example, fashioned a notorious distinction between the Hutu and Tutsi tribes which after their departure ensured the genocide witnessed in Rwanda.

Then of course, by the use of the most lethal weapon of division—**language**— the Europeans dismembered Africa into a sustained political, social, economic and cultural Babel which would always be pulled apart into three main directions—English, French or Portuguese, depending on which country was the former colonial power. Simultaneously, by forcing their respective languages on colonised Black people, they ensured a bizarre form of unity through which partitioned African peoples are forced to identify more with those who colonised them than with fellow Africans.

The effects are endemic, sustained and involuntarily devastating. The African businessman in English speaking Malawi will find it easier to do business in far away United Kingdom than in neighbouring Mozambique, while his Mozambican counterpart will find it easier to trade in Lisbon, Portugal, thousands of miles away and across seas than in Blantyre, only a few hundred miles away! Congolese Africans will find it easier to deal with France than with Angola right next door. The economic losses to Black people resulting from these grotesque divisions are enormous!

In Yamassoukro, Ivory Coast, a few years ago, I attended a workshop of African ecclesiastical leaders in which men of the cloth were firmly divided into three opinions which were determined not by the issues, but by whether the African nation they came from was Anglophone, Francophone or Lusophone. You see, the colonial Babel does not exempt even the church. Never mind the fact that people of the same tribe divided between Zambia and Congo regard themselves as 'English' and 'French' respectively—their cultural environment also suffers alienation from each other.

I understand fully the stance of former White Europeans in countries for example like South Africa who have real commitment to Africa and regard themselves as African in an African 'rainbow' nation. Yet because of the bizarre effects of colonial division, the colour Black, coming from any place outside the artificial colonial borders, has no place in the rainbow—denied not by White people, but by fellow Black people who regard their fellow Africans as stark foreigners. In recent bouts of the madness born of these fostered divisions, Africans in South Africa demonstrated such passionate hatred and hostility to fellow Africans from outside the colonial drawn borders that they literally set fellow Africans on fire. Black children were made to watch this blood thirsty spectacle, entrenching a legacy of division into future generations of Black People.

Some clever White intellectuals, sensing these attacks as the successful harvest of the seeds of division sown among Africans by their progenitors, swiftly and cunningly christened this fraternal blood-letting of Bantu blood as "xenophobia". Ironically the true meaning of that word is "aversion to anything that is foreign or does not look like you". There is really no strangeness between two Black people. The right term for it, heavy with irony and contradiction though it may be, is Afro-phobia—Africans loathing Africans. Someday, the Black People of Africa will wake up to the fact that their woes proceed from chronic shared poverty which is a direct result of the economic dispossession by White colonialism common to all their ancestors. The tragedy of it all is that many influential political, religious, social and intellectual Black leaders are silent on Afro-phobia, choosing rather to make statements about issues in far off lands, while there is a desperate need to educate Black people at home and on the continent about the importance of overcoming such divisions fostered on them by their former masters.

There is something definitely unique about South Africa. We must celebrate Nelson Mandela's distinguished success through his and others' sacrificial struggle to liberate South Africa from apartheid and to create a Rainbow Nation in which people of different origins and colours now dwell in harmony.

However, the political leaders of South Africa must not lose sight of a parallel and more important mission they must pursue—the struggle to lift up the overwhelming masses of Black Africans in and outside the colonially drawn borders to their place of economic, political and social dignity and competitiveness.

Increasingly, it appears that the faintest colour on the rainbow tapestry of growing South African economic and social advantage is the colour that should by right be the most visible of all—the colour Black. Dear South Africa, we need a rainbow indeed, but with a dominant broad swathe of brilliant Black. Without this, the rainbow will be doomed to a red diffusion of fresh revolution. When the Black

People of Africa are raised into their proper place, their dignity and competitiveness based on self-realisation will assure the future of the rainbow.

There are two major doctrines which political leaders owe Black Africans—the doctrine of Affirmation and the doctrine of African Unity. Yes, affirmation. For how can we expect that a people humiliated, oppressed and disadvantaged for four hundred years only on the basis of their Black skin can over the space of a couple of decades suddenly stand as psychological equals side by side with other colours in the rainbow? There is need for our political leaders to set out on a multi-faceted and very robust affirmation of Black People, including educational programs of psychological re-orientation that build up confidence in Africanness. It is a political mistake to react mutely when White students make Black cleaners eat food which they have urinated on, film it all and declare that they did it to show what they think of Black People. Things like this mirror much greater vulnerabilities for the Black People in many areas of the rainbow.

And yes, the doctrine of African Unity. What makes South Africa so special is that as the last liberated piece of the African continent, it is also endowed with great economic clout and international competitiveness. It is the great hope of African resurgence through African Unity. There is a school of thought that goes like this: *South Africa, you are strong, rich and successful unlike all those impoverished failed African nations to the north who are flooding you with their destitute people. Abandon them, identify with, and take your place in the developed world.*

There is unspeakable folly in this school of thought which has stretched its tentacles even into the hearts and minds of poor Africans in South Africa who resent other poor Africans from the North whom they perceive as coming to finish their jobs and resources. The truth of course is that these are just poor Black People come to share a common poverty which originated from the same source—historical White domination of Black People.

I once had the privilege of pointing out to a consultative gathering of Southern African Presidents that the term 'squatter' in a politically independent Southern Africa is mainly reserved for Black Africans who eke out a piteous living be it in Kibera Nairobi, Hatcliffe Harare, Old Naledi Gaborone or Diepsloot Johannesburg. The poverty in a Nigerian, Somali, Mozambican, Zimbabwean, Congolese, Malawian or South African shanty settlement is frighteningly identical. It should not be rocket science for African political leaders to realise that the most powerful tool for lifting up these Black People, united by their poverty, is to unite them to rise up as one People, one Africa in their struggle for the dignity, prosperity and competitiveness of a common African Village.

It is very short sighted for Africans in the South to be blinded by the temporary seeming state of deprivation in other African nations. Did not the British, the French, the Belgians, the Germans gain their strong economic positions by seeing beyond the surface into the potential wealth that lay in seemingly poor African lands and peoples? They quickly assimilated with these seemingly poor tribes, albeit through the predator culture of colonialism—and gained unspeakable wealth through African material and coerced human resources.

How much more should South Africa and other African nations, coming from the common African identity and brotherhood, take up the challenge of opening up our artificial borders, assimilating strategically and exploiting the Continent's potential as one? A fresh exodus of African resources is taking place under our noses, for example to Eastern nations, while African political leaders dither on the issue of African unity and fuel an almost neo-tribalistic defunct nationalism within borders drawn by colonial masters.

It was heartening in the last half of the twentieth century to witness the rise of the doctrine of Pan Africanism through political prophets such as Kwame

Nkrumah and others. It was an inspiration to see one part of Africa after another gain freedom with African Unity as part of their vision. Nothing compares to the actions for African Unity that spoke louder than words as parts of Africa that had gained freedom sacrificially hosted refugees and Liberation Movements from other parts of Africa that had not yet attained their liberation, all the time fuelled by the correct realisation that Africa was not free until every part of the continent was free.

And last to gain this freedom with the unwavering support of seemingly poor parts of Africa was South Africa, symbolically placed geographically as the feet on which the rest of the continent of Africa stands.

It has been heart-warming to see South African leaders over the past decade utilise their advantage to bring peace and other initiatives to other African nations and open South Africa up to Africans from other parts of the continent. From Sudan to Burundi, from Corte d'Ivoire to Zimbabwe, South African political leaders have laboured to pacify the continent. And this is as it should be because the highest and most sacred duty of an African leader is to know that the People of Africa are one.

And this is why South Africa and all Africa should not now be deceived into dropping the ball. It is time to train the Peoples of Africa into a new strategic synergy. A part of Africa which may not have as yet apparent wealth may excel in ideas and resources. For example parts of Africa in which Black People have had political independence for some time have provided Black People with time to go through invaluable training in the struggle to take resources or enterprise under hard conditions. A Somali Black kiosk business owner has invaluable lessons for the Black South African aspiring kiosk owner who is finding it near impossible to break through in a White dominated economy. The Black Zimbabwean farmer or small mine claim owner could inspire his

Black brother in South Africa to whom the handling of gold or diamonds by himself as a Black owner may seem unreal.

It is the Black South African investor who must go to Congo or Zambia, Mozambique or Zimbabwe, Nigeria or Tanzania and synergise with fellow Africans there to exploit the abundant resources and opportunities. Yet without training our people into a new ideology of African unity, we will watch the Chinese, Whites and other people exploit these opportunities while Black People major on a self-destructive afro-phobia.

It is time therefore for the African political leader to embark on an impassioned mission to teach African People the vital need for them to understand and embrace their oneness throughout the continent and to initiate among them Indabas for synergy and networking. The people will not get there by themselves. They need the focussed guidance of enlightened political leaders.

If the revelation of African Unity were more meaningfully communicated by African politicians, Africans all over the continent and beyond would be consulting and working fraternally together resulting in a new age of self-empowerment by Black People.

Although I have put great demand on the African politician, African leaders in every field must take up the task of building the concept of African Unity in the hearts and minds of Africans everywhere. And this applies also to the African outside the continent be it the African American, the African in the Indies, Caribbean or Europe. A great and positive phenomenon of our time has been the rise and elevation of Black Leaders into prominence at an international level. Some of these Prophets, such as Dr. Martin Luther King, Jr., Malcolm X, Bantu Steven Biko and others had to pay the ultimate price for their struggle for the uplifting of Black People.

The present generation of Black Leaders whose voices have earned the attention of the world must not be side-tracked by premature international accolades to think that their mission among the Black People has been accomplished. From legendary liberators and achievers like Mandela, Kaunda, Mbeki, Chissano and others, to sitting Presidents like Zuma, Banda, Dos Santos, Bingu wa Mutharika, Kikwete, Obama, Kagame, Pohamba, Mugabe, Museveni and others, to prominent clergy like Archbishop Tutu, Rev. Jesse Jackson, Rev. Andrew Young and others, as well as from a young generation of Black Leaders must rise renewed initiatives and a shrill voice for the unity, dignity and competitiveness of Black People worldwide.

One cannot help wincing in pain as many of these voices are lost through a false assumption that mission is accomplished and they can now retire or ascend to the prestige of becoming messiahs of all people worldwide. There are forces in this world that have a deeply vested interest in deceiving or dignifying leaders of Black People into this kind of tragic irrelevance. The assassin's bullet has always been very brutally precise with Black Leaders with the right message. The new and golden bullet is the reward of international prestige, and it is just as accurate.

I hope I have not been presumptuous in including President Barack Obama, the first Black President of the United States of America, among African leaders. I was truly impressed by the way this extraordinary African-American man openly celebrated his African origins before America and the world, both in his writings and by his celebrated 'pilgrimages' to Africa before he came into power. In this man's family comes a confluence of every concept of the African holocaust through the slave trade and colonialism. His grandfather was a detainee in the infamous British detention and torture camps in Kenya where thankfully he was not castrated as others were. His wife hails from Africans uprooted to America through the slave trade.

Obama has by divine providence ascended to arguably the most powerful political office in the world. A slave has become a king, and Black people from among whom he hails are anxiously waiting to see what his voice and contribution on behalf of Black and African people is going to be. While Irish Presidents like Bill Clinton can look back with pride at the way they used this high office to help the Irish in their peace process, Obama does not seem to be yet on course to raise a meaningful word or finger towards causes crucial to the African people, such as for example African Unity or the rehabilitation of Black People's minds and economies from the traumas of the holocaust. He has been content to rehash lectures of former colonial Western leaders to African leaders struggling against staggering odds on the subject of corruption and incompetence, and to tread a path of sanctions, bombs and disregard of the views of African leaders that is embarrassing in its lack of both imagination and originality.

President Obama should be having a special multi-million dollar task force dedicated to engaging and empowering the African Union and African leaders. He is in an advantaged position to examine the failure of imposition of un-adapted Western democracy models on African nations which are the root causes of many electoral and civil conflicts. It would be so energising to Africa to see him inviting clusters of African leaders for consultation on African problems in the White House rather than focussing entirely on the Semitic tribes of the Middle East.

The voice of the African Union on African countries such as Libya should be more important to him than the voice of the Arab League. The Arabs advised Obama to bomb Libya in Africa and not Yemen or Bahrain in Arab lands for identical problems. Ironically, this Arab-Western symphony was the engine of the African Slave Trade. For less than the cost of one tomahawk cruise missile Obama could achieve major strides towards inspiring African Unity and dignity. I hope the President will have a change of heart, for I can see coming White

American Presidents ignoring or bombing Africa in the name of his example. Will it be conscionable for Obama to leave office with an African record bettered by George Bush?

Black People's intellectual leaders have not been exempted from this conspiracy of misdirection. Africa and Black People worldwide have already suffered from a dearth of intellectual thought on which they could, like other Peoples, found their identity, politics, competitiveness and unity. The Black intellectual is burning out his energies on parroting over-subscribed themes of Western democracy and sexual rights instead of drawing creative themes for Black People from the rich social, cultural and political heritage of the amazing paradigm of African consensus. If this unfortunate trend continues, history will record our times as a ridiculous era of African intellectual slavery.

No one notices that the reason African youth is distinguishing itself by lack of unique direction is the sheer absence of a body of distinct African intellectual thought. While the cheques which foreign non-government organisations pay for papers promoting Western ideas are handsome, it is time for Black intellectuals to abandon the role of Prophets for hire and return to the place of relevance to their own People. Prime to this relevance should be cutting edge theses on the critical theme of African Unity.

The visionaries whose dreams gave birth to the political liberation Africa has experienced, saw the liberation and uniting of Africa as one and the same Dream. Kwame Nkrumah, founding President of the first free African nation, Ghana, spoke of the United Nations of Africa, and gave momentum to co-operation of African nations to liberate the whole continent together by declaring that the liberation of Africa would be meaningless until every country on the continent was set free. The Organisation of African Unity, now the African Union, was organised to ultimately mould Africa into one economic and political entity.

This dream should be held sacred by all Black people and should never be trivialized. It holds in it the surest promise of dignity and competitiveness for African people.

To understand this, we must have a clear world view. The reality of the world is that those who are unable to form a powerful united front will ultimately have to submit themselves to one powerful bloc or other because of economic and military realities. During the cold war African nations were turned into an ideological playground of big powers. They ended up variously adopting political systems irrelevant to African needs, instead of crafting a system relevant to Africans.

Present realities also point towards an imminent volunteered re-colonization of African countries under those who have built strong united blocs or nations, unless the continent's leaders embark on an urgent and aggressive initiative towards comprehensive unity.

Africans deserve an identity, presence and significance that is able to support integrity, dignity and self-determination. The present situation where former colonial masters police African countries and even national constitutions have to be drawn up with outrageously irrelevant clauses aped to please big nations, while bereft of any African values is a one way ticket to a new slavery.

African political leaders must wake up to the fact that the present misguided doctrine of seeking to be in rhythm with an international community made up of blocs which have through unity built themselves into strong entities, while African nations themselves have not built themselves to the same or greater strength through African Unity—is tantamount to again leaving Africa armed with bows and arrows—this time ideological bows and arrows—in a world which is on every side armed with the advanced ideological weaponry of unity.

In our lifetime, nations are deliberately emerging in significance. It is critical that an African significance emerge. It is the one significance glaringly lagging behind, and if this continues Black people shall once again be taken serious advantage of. Instead of assimilating with the world, Africa should urgently close itself in and map out and implement its Unity so that it may not continue to be a rabbit among beasts of prey.

A united Africa would easily acquire or even dictate terms of trade favourable to itself on the world market. The present situation where Africa holds a lion's share of resources while only being able to reap a chicken's portion when these resources are traded, proceeds chiefly from one source—the disunity of African nations. A misguided and short sighted fractured nationalism in Africa has some nations of the world laughing all the way to the bank at the expense of African people. History will not honour Africa's present leadership if they continue to focus on preserving these small principalities. History will hail them as men and women of foresight if they change direction and boldly unite the African continent.

Uniting the nations of Africa is not at all a complex issue. There are many factors that will come to their help if the continent's leaders assume real leadership in uniting Africa. Not least of these factors is the oneness and goodwill that exists among the African people themselves. Left to themselves, they will welcome, mingle and assimilate with one another quite easily. I have been to almost every African nation south of the Sahara and have never felt like a visitor anywhere. When the politicians finally roll up their sleeves and unite the continent, they will discover that the people are way ahead of them.

There are some simple steps that Africans can take in order to build momentum towards African unity. The formation of the African Union, the African Parliament and regional politico—economic blocks such as the Southern African

Development Community, Economic Community of West African States, East African Community, Preferential Trade Area, and so on, is a resounding step in the right direction. These organisations must be taken seriously and be given teeth to aggressively formulate and pursue programs that will enhance African Unity.

The African Union in particular needs to be given an irreversible and aggressive mandate to unite Africa and to 'market' the concept of African Unity aggressively all over the continent. Pan African visionaries like former South African President Thabo Mbeki must not be buried in the graveyard of local South African politics, but in the context of the African Union, must be mandated to use their extraordinary gifts and experience to formulate, steer and aggressively implement an incisive program for a United Africa.

'One Africa' is a concept every African must be endeared to, the children and the youth in particular. Certain core educational curricula can be introduced to make African Education uniform in key areas. An African National Anthem is long overdue. This is a powerful but uncomplicated symbol which could easily foster a sense of African oneness and patriotism. One African nation which realised its freedom later than most African nations is Namibia. Older African nations have much to learn from the way this younger sibling has kept fresh and upheld values of African Unity concerning which some African nations appear to be suffering from amnesia. In Namibia, for example, the African National Anthem is sung at state and important occasions together with the local anthem. This should urgently be emulated by other African nations.

A simple but crucial way to foster the spirit of African Unity in the hearts of African people everywhere is for the African Union to start aggressive programs targeted at caring for African people throughout the continent, particularly in times of disasters such as floods, earthquakes, droughts, displacement and famine. Even now it is quite embarrassing that when disasters strike African people, Africa is conspicuous by its absence in emergency relief programs while particularly western nations are very high in their profile as the relief providers. This stereotype has a negative impact on the minds of Black people.

The African Union needs to speedily set-up a high powered disaster relief department and must be first to react in all disasters on the continent, and in-fact take leadership in these programs. It will be heartening in the future to see African Union helicopters rescuing people in floods and A.U cargo planes arrive timeously with food and medical relief.

This is in fact a culture which Africa desperately needs to train her children and people into. In western nations for instance, even children are heavily conscientised to respond to needs around the world through collections and so forth. It is amazing how in African nations there are almost no programs to mobilise people to help in disasters even in neighbouring countries. This is an issue needing urgent attention at every level-from the family to the school to the government there must be aggressive programs to mobilise African people to care for African and other people in time of need.

It is time to mandate, convene and train a dedicated and standing Pan-African Military force. Development of African defence industries with their own integrity is also an urgent imperative. Apart from economy, there is nothing more important to the security, integrity, stature and wholesomeness of a people than a credible military force. Individual African countries may not alone be able to marshal a military force worth of respect, but if Africa can come together in this field, a formidable army with strategic bases and worthy of respect can be built in a matter of months. The present embarrassing reality is that strong nations in the world regard the whole of Africa as a military joke, yet there are small nations in this world which have developed their defences to a place worthy of healthy respect, even by military super powers.

One of Africa's most visionary leaders was Mwalimu Julius Nyerere. This great man boldly sought a path of economic self-reliance, cultural revolution and identity for African people. His efforts have borne far reaching and evident fruit. When I have visited Tanzania, I have always been deeply touched by its Black people's deep sense of patriotism, self-reliance, dignity, creativeness, self-confidence and a sheer love for Africa. Though Tanzania faces the battle of lifting up its people economically, its people have largely stayed in Tanzania to win their economic war at home rather than become economic refugees. Tanzania remains one of the best positioned countries for indigenous African innovativeness.

A very important achievement of the Mwalimu was to adopt Swahili, the most widely spoken indigenous language in Africa, as Tanzania's primary language. In the schools, even science is taught in Swahili. He had grasped the fact that language is an important key to the distinction, unity, dignity and self determination of a people. Up to now, one of the most embarrassing things on international forums is to hear Arabs, Chinese, Europeans and others give addresses in their own languages, while Africans speak in a concoction of colonial languages, sort of 'his master's voice'.

The Mwalimu was right. We need to urgently adopt one African language and begin to teach it in every African school. Swahili is best placed for this, or the African Union can commission a team of linguists to construct a language out of the beautiful linguistic foundation of African languages. A single language will be the most powerful tool for uniting the continent.

The Chinese deliberately took the radical step not too long ago in history, of re-developing their language with Chinese terms invented to replace every

English scientific, medical, economic or mathematical term. The impact of this was that these sciences became a natural part of their culture and it made a huge contribution to their indigenous progress in science and technology. Similarly, the new Jewish nation as late as the twentieth century revived classical Hebrew, practically dead for thousands of years, coined new Hebrew words for every technology, even the fountain pen, and made it the official language of their nation today. Africa urgently needs to take a step like this. Though inconvenient in the beginning, the rewards will dwarf the inconvenience.

The unity of Africans must include a fresh initiative to foster oneness between Africans on the Continent and Africans historically removed to far off lands, be it voluntarily or by force. This is why strong ties must again be built between Africa and such groups as African Americans, Africans in the Caribbean, United Kingdom, Europe and other parts of the world. The historical positioning of African people in many parts of the world holds vast potential for the social, political, cultural and economic advantage for Black people everywhere, provided a new unity is built among them.

This issue, the issue of African Unity, One Africa, is the issue on which Black intellectuals should be focussing. Young Africans should be fired up with the agenda of African Unity. Editors should be seriously weighting their publications with this issue, and establishing a new standard upon which politicians and their programs should be judged—relevance to African Unity. Every person and institution of influence should be weighing in on this issue. The clergy need to be shrill in their calls for the unity of Black people. Above all, African governments and politicians all over the world should work tirelessly towards the unity of Black people.

African Unity is the underestimated key to the greatness of Black people worldwide. It is the achievement of African unity that will lead other nations of the world, even the Almighty Himself, to look at last at Black People with awe and respect and say:

> *Behold the Africans are **one**, and they all have one language, and now nothing will be restrained from them, which they have imagined to do.*

African voices continue to speak to the generations of Africa

Herbert Chitepo, 1923-1975
Brilliant intellectual and proponent of strategic philosophies for independence and self-reliance by Black people. Led the Zimbabwe liberation movement ZANU until 1975 assassination.

Chapter 6

Bantu Steven Biko

Through his philosophy of Black Consciousness Bantu Steven Biko inspired a new thinking in the minds of Black people to struggle for their own economic emancipation.

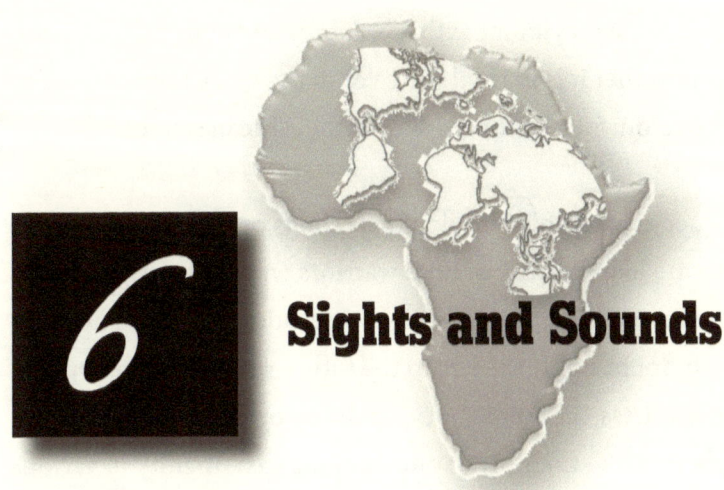

6 Sights and Sounds

*B*lack People are tired of being spectators of a game they should be playing.

Bantu Steven Biko

*I*t is amazing how during the last quarter of the twentieth century, breakthroughs in communication technologies began to bring literally the whole world into our living rooms through satellite television. I still remember the time when one pioneering leading network, Cable News Network, commonly known as CNN, was launched and began to bring events happening in many parts of the world live onto our television sets.

Someone at CNN once came up with a fascinating concept which they called *Sights and Sounds. Sights and Sounds of Egypt*-then they would show clips of interesting and attractive scenes from Egypt. It would give you the impression of a thirty-second visit to whatever country they showed.

Travelling in various parts of the African continent, there is a Sight and Sound that never ceases to grab my attention and to fill my heart with warmth in a way I am sure it would yours. It is a sight vibrant with life, energy and above all potential, hope and promise. Whether it is in rural Africa or in the cities I never cease to be captivated by the colourful sight of children in the African school.

As they stand in order at assembly and sing their songs or recite their prayers they always look to me like an army of little warriors waiting to wage war for African identity and competitiveness in years and decades to come. The mind of the Black child no doubt holds the key to the future rise of Black people to that level of competitiveness-economic, social, political or otherwise which will enable Black people to make their own contributions to humanity in various fields. This is why everyone who cares for the future success of Black people must prioritise the accurate and relevant education and training of the young generation. This education and training must be in ways that will set them free from the deceptions which were incorporated in their education in the past and empower them with strategic knowledge and wisdom thus far withheld from them which will enable them to hold their own in the "dog eat dog" global economic village.

Some years ago I was holding a conference in a vibrant East African capital. I watched the *national* evening newscast in my hotel room and saw a news clip which caused me anxiety for many years. The president of the nation was visiting one of the beautiful schools and took time to give a motivational talk to those immaculately uniformed children. The part of his speech which the broadcaster chose to highlight went as follows; *'You are very fortunate to have the opportunity to be in this school. You must study hard and especially, you must learn English, French, German and other European languages. This is because the English, the French, the Germans and other Europeans will come here and open their businesses. They will need people who know their languages to work for them, so you will get a job.'* The president drew applause from both staff and students for this piece of generational 'wisdom'.

The most important contest among nations in the global village has always been the competition for resources and wealth. On this economic playing field, the field where principals in industry, commerce—business, trade, mining, agriculture, technology, cyber-trade and so on—are the clear winners, the African president was advocating for the training of black children to fill only the role of employees who would assist foreigners to become the dominant players in the game of exploiting the economic resources of Africa. And the trainers, the teachers, were applauding.

To all parents, government and other education departments and institutions, trainers, educators and stewards of Black children and youth everywhere, must arise a clear and unequivocal revelation that the Black child must, of critical necessity be trained to become a principal player on the national and global economic playing field. If this is not done, future generations of Black people will, just like present and past generations, be condemned to be spectators in the most important game they should be playing—the game of becoming the principal wealth builders and owners of the economic and financial resources of their nations, and of the world.

It is clear that the Black people everywhere remain at the bottom of the global economic food chain. This is not a natural or providential phenomenon. It was deliberately orchestrated by those who, through the plunder of slavery and colonialism, systematically dispossessed the progenitors of Black people. The strategy which was designed to perpetuate this dispossession of Black people even after political independence was to deliberately design for them systems of education and training through which they could only see themselves as workers for, or employees of economic principals, largely of people of other colours. I can understand the generational 'wisdom' of the African president. He grew up in a context where the prescribed way for a Black person to address any white man, even on the street, was *baas* or *boss*. To the present day in some

African dialects the phrase, *"my white person"* is the accepted euphemism for, *"my employer"*. *Worse still, some African dialects use the same word for "God" and "white man".*

The Black political leader needs to realise that political liberation means nothing without economic emancipation. And since the shackles that were used to train Black people to accept a subservient role in economy are mental shackles, drastic measures must be taken to undo those shackles through relevant education and training. No amount of government grants or relief and charity programs will be able to elevate economically a person who in his mind sees himself as unable, undeserving or unfit to be an aggressive principal player in wealth creation. This is why a new sound must be added to the sights and sounds of the school, society and nation—the voice of well thought economic re-education and re-training of the minds of young Black people.

This financial and economic re-education and retraining is an extremely urgent matter. Black leaders, people and nations are content to watch in idle apathy while people of other colours who were also victims of oppression and dispossession are aggressively re-asserting themselves on the global economic playing field. Black people have not yet entered this race, but are content to, at best, survive on whatever crumbs will fall to them from the sumptuous tables of those who through history focussed on fighting by fair means or foul for their own place of economic advantage. There is simply no case for Black nations to accept the fact that, for example, formerly impoverished Eastern peoples must overtake us economically while we watch passively from the spectators' gallery, soon to become the beggar's gallery! The future global economic map is being re-drawn under our noses. There are no favours. Any people who want a place at this economic table must fight for their own space. Unlike the past, any future position at the bottom of the global food chain will be voluntary.

I feel persuaded that Africans are God's favourite people. Before you dismiss this statement, consider that the bulk of the world's resources for wealth building—be it minerals, wild life, fertile land, vegetation,—the list goes on—were deposited at creation in Africa. Colonial and slave trading nations enriched themselves through the rape of African natural resources and the abuse of African human labour resources. Black people can be excused for this era of dispossession by force. But what excuse is there for the present culture of continuing to watch other peoples come and take advantage of natural resources which Black people can so easily exploit, process and add value to themselves and then use to compete with as exports on the global economic playing field? If African leaders and people can begin to think in this way, it won't be long before the tables are turned and the world looks to Africa for economic aid. Black people must assume a new determination to enrich themselves with Africa's resources and industriousness in the same way they enriched those who plundered them in the past.

There are three simple messages which it is imperative for this economic education and training to contain. The first message to the Black person and to the Black child must be the message of **ownership**. When Black people everywhere were dispossessed through slavery and colonialism, this was done through violent plunder followed by a sustained programme of forced expropriation. Through this, it was demonstrated to the Black person that he had no right to ownership of any meaningful material resource in the land bequeathed to him by his ancestors.

In the case of slavery which is the root of the present day poverty of such Diaspora Black people as African Americans and others, it was violently demonstrated to the Black person that he did not own even himself nor his children. Even his wife could be raped by the slave owner at will. His labour for the master was not remunerated. In the case of colonialism the unfortunate

Black people on the African continent were violently dispossessed of any fertile or productive land and even livestock. Relegated to barren tracts of land, they were employed for meagre wages to do the bulk of the work needed for the colonial master to exploit for his own profit the resources of the land of the birth right of the colonised.

The mind of the Black person was, through this trauma sustained for four hundred years, trained to accept that he really had no right to ownership of wealth and resources even on his own continent. Even today, the propensity of Black people to be objects of charity, to receive rather than to give, is rooted in the deep psychological trauma of years in which they could not own anything except that permitted, left over or handed to them by the white master. It is this unfortunate heritage which makes it very difficult for the Black person to visualise or take for granted his right to ownership of wealth and resources— even of good things which people of other colours consider as necessities. In many Black families the acquisition of even a small automobile is considered as a monumental achievement for which the entire village must gather for celebration. Yet it is just a simple necessity for transportation.

It is for this reason that the mind of the Black young person must be radically retrained and re-educated. He must be made to understand that he has the right to ownership of resources and a key role in the creation of wealth in the global village, and especially in his own land. In the political arena, this re-training needs to be underlined by programs which facilitate access to resources for the purpose of wealth creation for disadvantaged Black people. Though this will never amount to the reparations which should have been done to restore the economic foundations of Black people, it will be a right, albeit small, step in the right direction. Coupled with this must be energetic training programs in wealth creation and educational modules in economic ideological re-orientation.

Civil society, whose unwitting message to the Black person has by and large been a message that he must be a perpetual object of charity needs as well to redirect its efforts and message to facilitating access to resources meant for wealth creation, and means of production for Black people. Simple modules on wealth creation and entrepreneurship for young people will achieve much more sustainable development than endless hand outs of consumables. The continuous stereotyping of Black people by civil society as the perpetual poor and needy of the earth is doing more harm than good. Though it jerks tears which lead people to fill the coffers of charitable organisations, it needs to be urgently replaced with concepts which place a definitive accent on facilitating the ascent of Black people to the culture of indigenous wealth creation.

Religious teaching must also be faithful to the clear Divine emphasis that the poor and oppressed must be tutored and led into economic exoduses, fighting all odds in order to enter into material promised lands in which they will in Deuteronomic fashion "multiply flocks, dig brass and build goodly houses and dwell in them while eating bread without scarceness."

In fact one fundamental issue in which it is critical to re-train, re-educate and inspire the minds of Black young people is the issue of ownership of the **land**. A direct result of the strategic damage inflicted by slavery and colonialism upon the minds of Black people in general, and Black young people in particular, is apathy and disinterest towards land ownership, especially rural and farm land ownership. Land is the root and foundation of all wealth. Whether it is precious metals such as platinum, gold and silver, or precious stones such as diamonds, industrial raw materials such as chrome, copper and iron, or food stuffs such as corn, meat, and vegetables, or materials for manufacturing furniture and clothing such as wool, cotton and timber-all wealth originates in the land. It is in fact rural resources which build cities. Most of the African cities we have so far seen were created under colonialism from rural resources. We keenly await the rise of new cities, created and built in rural areas by a new generation of free Black people with an understanding of the value and potential of land.

This is why the white colonisers of Africa targeted land above anything else and forcibly removed Black indigenous owners from large fertile and mineral rich tracts of land, resettling them in barren and semi-arid areas. This assured a solid economic foundation for white people for generations to come. Simultaneously it built revulsion towards land within Black people, as their only understanding of land was the barren tracts into which they were crowded by force. This explains the urban myth in the minds of Black people in which the thinking is that the only way to get money or wealth is to migrate to the cities and compete, most of the time in dire poverty and heart breaking living conditions, for scant and unrewarding employment opportunities. Ironically this employment will come from people who built financial empires using resources from land.

African governments must put at the top of their agendas the issue of empowering the formerly dispossessed Black people by programs of meaningful land redistribution in which fertile and mineral rich land is restored to the Black people. Simultaneously, young Black minds need to be empowered by being taught the value of land ownership and the skills to extract mineral, agricultural and other forms of wealth from the land. Every Black person must seek to own and develop a piece of rural land—even land in the barren rural areas must not be abandoned. In lands like Israel the Jews have converted the desert into incredible orchards and farm land. Africa must prioritise training Black people in modern technologies that make land productive. The young Black person must be inspired to go back to the land-to develop, farm and mine it. Future genuinely African cities will be developed through rural development. This is a more strategic path than continuing directing our young people into urban areas which have already been over exploited. Through engaging the land,

Black young people will create employment, rather than continue to live in the frustration of seeking it.

The second message which needs to be emphasised in the economic education and re-training of Black young people is the message of *aggressive creativity and initiative*. Regaining economic space is going to require unfettered creativity, initiative and aggressiveness. Young Black people must be woken up to the fact that the culture of the global village is that resources, wealth and space to build wealth must be fiercely competed for or fought for.

Although during the season of Black people's struggles for political liberation, armed aggression was at times necessary to liberate Black people, the aggression needed in the battle for wealth and resources is no longer physical aggression. It is mental creativity, innovation and initiative. These are the weapons needed for the second Liberation Struggle of Black People—an Economic Liberation Struggle. This struggle is far harder than the political one, and the truth is that Black National leaders are under unbearable pressure to shy away from this struggle and succumb to the forces of world economic domination of Africa.

During the long season of oppression, Black people lost their power to dream, to initiate and to create. You see, dreams are for free people—oppressed people's power to dream was drowned in a flood of nightmare realities. As their raw materials were shipped out to be processed in the lands of their colonisers, the concept of value addition to their own raw materials through local processing and manufacturing was erased from the minds of Black people. Simultaneously, the culture of creativity and initiative was destroyed as dispossession rendered these concepts irrelevant, and servitude gave birth to a deep inferiority complex which made Black people look down on anything of their own creation. Even tasty and nutritious indigenous foods were discarded in favour of the 'prestige' of often unhealthy and tasteless Western foods. The pervasive portrait of the

White person as the business owner made the vision of himself as the initiator of business faint in the mind of the Black person.

The young Black person must now be taught and trained to a new understanding that he or she must become the leader and initiator in wealth creation through dreams, ideas and innovation of his own creation. The young Black person must embrace his or her new role as combatant on behalf of all Black people on the battle field of wealth creation. This must start with the embracing of a new culture in which Black people believe in their own products and process and add value through manufacturing and other industries and technologies to their own resources and raw materials.

It is embarrassing that entrepreneurs will come all the way from Europe and create a fried chicken business using the same cockerel which Black people are regarding as an alarm clock to wake them up in the morning. They will sell it to the Portuguese owner of a Nandos outlet, who will add value to it simply by cutting it into pieces and spicing and grilling it, then selling small pieces of it to the very same Black people he bought it from at a higher price per piece than the whole cockerel! The Black man is employed by a White man who comes and starts a furniture business by cutting and milling the same tree which the Black man saw only as the source of a shade to sit under. African diamonds don't have to be cut in Brussels or abroad, neither do African people have to import from Europe garments made from their own exports of cotton. The African tantalite can be used to make micro-chips and cell phones in Black countries rather than be exported raw to the world.

Knowledge and information coupled to amazingly simple and available technologies have become the most powerful tools of trade and wealth creation in the global village. Black governments and communities must spare no resource or effort in building up the most modern communication highway infrastructures possible. Nor should they spare energy and resources in training Black children all the way down to the village school in the use of such technologies as the internet, and especially their use in trade and business. All the time an awareness must be aggressively built in young Black people that international trade, wealth creation and economic achievement is accessible to them and must be aggressively embraced as a challenge.

Both in the Diaspora and on the African continent there is a growing pool of Black entrepreneurs who are emerging and making a meaningful impact in the global village, and a few authors and publications have taken the noble step of chronicling their stories. Such books and publications need to be given wide exposure and to be added into the curricula and libraries of Black educational institutions. Successful Black entrepreneurs need to redouble efforts to conduct motivational workshops in schools, colleges and young people's institutions, and the media needs to keep them visible to young people.

The third message which needs to be loudly proclaimed to the Black young person is the simple message of *competence* that propelled the first Black and relatively young man into the presidency of the United States of America—*yes we can!* In other words, contrary to the stereotypes, *yes, Black person, Black young person, you are as capable, able and competent as anybody else to marshal resources and create wealth.*

The self-confidence of the Black person remains one of the most abiding casualties of the years of servitude, oppression and dispossession. For years, the Black person was assaulted with the message, *you cant do this, you cant do that.* It was in fact so sadistic that there were toilets which Black people could not enter under colonialism, not to mention areas they could not live in and business they could not do.

Self-confidence will not return spontaneously to Black people. It has to be aggressively rebuilt and reinforced by all right means possible. The Black young person needs to be re-educated and re-trained into a new mind of self-confidence and assumption of responsibility—*it is I who must create wealth and I have the ability to do so.* From the parents to the institutions, there must be a shrill voice that declares to the Black child, to the Black young person, *there is nothing good and profitable that is impossible for you to achieve!*

And, of course, my strongest word on the issue of marshalling resources for wealth—creation is to Black children and to young Black people themselves. If I could gather them all together I would tell them, *"The poverty you see in your parents in comparison to people of other colours does not mean that there is something wrong with you or your parents. It was deliberately created through the history of the plunder of Black people in Africa and all over the world over the past four hundred years through slavery and colonialism. Much of the wealth which you watch children of other colours enjoy was built on the foundation of the dispossession of your parents, grandparents and great-great grandparents.*

But through the bitter and sometimes bloody struggles of Black peoples all over the world for political liberation, the dividend of the struggle of your parents and grandparents, political freedom, justice and self-determination has come. The world has changed. On your shoulders now rests the responsibility for a new kind of struggle. You now have the responsibility and opportunity to mobilise resources, to build wealth and to change through your economic struggle the painful face of the poverty of Black people everywhere.

Yes, you may at times feel inadequate, timid and intimidated by the financial strength of people of other colours. You may even feel that you are not worthy to own the resources of your nation and of the world, or to create wealth. Fight and reject these feelings, for they were created in you by the many years of oppression which Black people suffered, oppression meant to create apathy in you towards ownership of resources and towards wealth creation.

Learn the history of the Black people and their struggles and embrace passionately the real truth: you have the God given right to own the resources of the land and to use them to create wealth for yourselves and for future generations. Learn the truth that you need to create your own dreams of wealth creation and aggressively compete for the world's wealth and resources through your own innovative enterprises. Embrace the ethic of hard work and defeat the temptation to be lazy—for with freedom comes responsibility.

Above all, reject the lie that you are incompetent or incapable, and raise the bold shout, YES I CAN! and there will be nothing impossible for you. You are able to compete with anybody in the global village in the game of wealth creation."

Somehow, I can hear the sights and sounds of an emerging prosperity of Black people. I hear the sights and sounds of these little future economic warriors in the African school. I hear the sights and sounds of them engaging the soil and going into farming and mining. I hear the sound of them developing and transforming rural areas of Africa which they have thus far shunned. I hear the sights and sounds of this live African terracotta army punching away on computer keyboards as they engage technology in the creation of numerous businesses and enterprises. I hear the sights and sounds of young Black people trading on the stock and financial markets. I hear the sights and sounds of this young generation of Black people creating industries and manufacturing enterprises and exporting competitively all over the world.

I hear the sights and sounds of the launchings of innovative inventions by young Black people. I hear the sights and sounds of money being traded in banks and financial institutions owned and run by these young Black people. I hear the sights and sounds of their executive jets landing and taking off at airports all over the world. I hear the sights and sounds of Black young people paying employees of their own and of other colours. I hear the sights and sounds of Black philanthropy as prosperous Black young people learn the freedom and joy of giving over receiving. I hear the sights and sounds of prosperous Black neighbourhoods, communities and nations of Black people.

Sights and sounds of a long overdue, desperately needed, urgently imperative and ultimately inevitable economic emancipation of Black people.

African voices continue to speak to the generations of Africa

George Padmore, *1903-1959*
A Trinidadian grandson of an Ashanti Warrior.
A leading Pan Africanist and campaigner for
the decolonization of Africa. He was advisor to
Kwame Nkrumah until his death in 1959.

Honours Roll: Some of Africa's Past and Present Heroes, Visionaries and Liberators

Kwame Nkrumah 1909-1972

Father of Pan Africanism and Ghana's Founding Father. "No amount of arguing about the so-called benefits of European rule can alter the fundamental right of Africans to order their own affairs."

Jomo Kenyatta 1894-1978

Pan Africanist, Founding Father of Kenya: "God said this is our land, land in which we flourish as people . . . we want our cattle to get fat on our land so that our children grow up in prosperity . . ."

Nehanda Charwe Nyakasikana

c1840-1898. She led Zimbabwe's First Chimurenga (Resistance) that inspired the Second Chimurenga which brought Zimbabwe to Independence in 1980. She told her colonial executioners, "My bones shall rise again."

Martin Luther King, Jr. 1929-1968.

African-American trail-blazer of the Civil Rights Movement which mobilized Black people to fight prejudice in order to take their rightful place in American society: "If a man hasn't discovered something that he will die for, he isn't fit to live."

Africa Fact

Africa is the most centrally located of all the continents. The prime meridian (Greenwich meridian) 0° cuts through the coast of West Africa while the Equator (latitude 0 degrees) also divides the continent into 2 equal parts North and South. Africa's centralized location in the world is an advantage.

Honours Roll: Some of Africa's Past and Present Heroes, Visionaries and Liberators

Bantu Steven Biko 1946-1977

Martyred Anti Apartheid Founder of the Black Consciousness Movement who asserted, "Black is beautiful": "What we need in our society is the power by us blacks to innovate. We have got the very system from which we can expand, . . ."

Patrice Lumumba, 1925-1961

Democratic Republic of Congo's visionary Leader, "We are going to keep watch over the lands of our country so that they truly profit her children. We are going to restore ancient laws and make new ones . . ." Assassinated with the collusion of Western Governments

Sekou Toure 1922-1984

Pan Africanist, Guinea's Founding Father, "We prefer freedom in poverty to riches in chains." Initiated programs to promote authentic African-ness and Black People's competitiveness

António Agostinho Neto, 1922-1979

Angola's Founding President. Chinua Achebe the Poet wrote of Neto, "I will celebrate The Man who rode a trinity Of awesome fates to the cause Of our trampled race! Thou Healer, Soldier, and Poet!"

Great African voices continue to speak to the generations of Africa

Rosa Parks, 1913-2005.
Ignited the American Civil Rights movement by defiantly riding a segregated bus, "I have learned over the years that when one's mind is made up, this diminishes fear . . . ."

Honours Roll: Some of Africa's Past and Present Heroes, Visionaries and Liberators

Julius Nyerere 1922-1999

Pan Africanist and Tanzania's Founding President,"[A] man is developing himself when he grows, or earns, enough to provide decent conditions for himself and his family; he is not being developed if someone gives him these things."

Amilcar Cabral 1924-1973

Visionary leader of the Liberation struggles in Guinea-Bissau and Cape Verde Islands, "Always bear in mind that the people are not fighting for ideas, for the things in anyone's head. They are fighting to win material benefits, to live better and in peace, to see their lives go forward, to guarantee the future of their children."

Harriet Tubman 1819-1913

Freed herself from slavery and organised 'The Underground Railroad' through which thousands of Southern slaves escaped to the North. Revered as a "Moses" among Black People

Cetshwayo kaMpande, 1827-1884

The last king of an independent Zulu nation. Mourning the loss of his men after defeating the British at the Battle of Isandlwana, 1879, "An assegai has been thrust into the belly of the nation, there are not enough tears to mourn for the dead."

Africa Fact

Africa is the most compact of all continents. It is as long as it is broad. It measures approximately 7,500 km from South to North as well as in its east-west extent. This is an advantage for travel and development.

Honours Roll: Some of Africa's Past and Present Heroes, Visionaries and Liberators

Kenneth Kaunda

Zambia's founding President. Worked for an independent Africa. "The inability of those in power to still the voices of their own consciences is the great force leading to change."

Samuel Nujoma

Founding President of Namibia, "What our people want is to be involved in the decision-making process and to actively participate in decisions which will ultimately affect them, . . . They then will take ownership."

Nelson Mandela

World renowned First President of Post Apartheid South Africa, "As we are liberated from our own fear, our presence automatically liberates others."

Thabo Mbeki

Visionary Pan African Statesman and South Africa's second post-Apartheid President. Continues to labour for Africa's peace, unity and competitiveness, "I am an African."

PATRIOTIC FRONT:
Robert Mugabe and the **late Joshua Nkomo** liberated Zimbabwe through twin armed struggles and went on to unite the nation under Mugabe presidency. President Mugabe maintains a fierce stand for Black economic empowerment and self-determination, "Africa is for Africans, pure and simple"

Great African voices continue to speak to the generations of Africa

Eduardo Mondlane, 1920-1969
Matyred co-founder and President of FRELIMO, the Front for the Liberation of Mozambique.

Honours Roll: Some of Africa's Past and Present Heroes, Visionaries and Liberators

Julius Malema, President of South African ANC Youth League, "We are in an economic struggle . . . Once that declaration is made, everyone will work towards economic emancipation. Our focus must be on economic freedom."

African Diamonds:

African visionaries see the land, wealth and resources of the continent and recognise the potential of the Continent's competitiveness through indigenous ownership and development of these resources.

Africas Visionaries uphold, as Steve Biko did, that the minds of Black People are the fertile ground in which the concepts of self-reliance, progress and productivity must first take shape.

Protest for land and housing in Cape Town

Africa Fact

Africa alone produces at least 50% of the diamonds and gold in the whole world. The rest of the countries around the world contribute to the remaining 50% of the production of these precious stones and metal.

Honours Roll: Some of Africa's Past and Present Heroes, Visionaries and Liberators

King Moshoeshoe 1 c1786-1870.

Warrior and diplomat king and founder of the Lesotho nation. He defeated both British and Boer invaders through shrewd military engagement and diplomacy to birth an African nation which has never been colonised, "Take me for all that I am together with the lice of my blanket but interfere not with my people for I shall remain their leader."

Samora Machel 1933-1986.

Mozambique's Founding President and Revolutionary Leader of FRELIMO Liberation army, "International solidarity is not an act of charity: It is an act of unity between allies fighting on different terrains toward the same objective. The foremost of these objectives is to aid the development of humanity to the highest level possible."

Seretse Khama 1921-1980.

Paramount Chief and Founding President of Botswana. He built the former British "Protectorate" into an independent nation, "A nation without a past is a lost nation, and a people without a past is a people without a soul"

King Sobhuza II, 1899-1982.

Warrior King and founder of the Kingdom of Swaziland which is counted amongst African nations today. He is remembered for his insistence on the maintenance of traditional tribal values at a time of colonial upheaval and domination

African voices continue to speak to the generations of Africa

Malcolm X, 1925-1965
Martyred champion of the struggle of Black People in America and beyond for their identity, dignity and self-determination.

Honours Roll: Some of Africa's Past and Present Heroes, Visionaries and Liberators

Winnie Madikizela Mandela.

Anti-Apartheid leader, politician and social activist: *"We want freedom in our lifetime. We want economic emancipation in our lifetime . . . ."*

Jesse L. Jackson.

Leading African American Civil Rights Activist and Baptist Minister. Founder of the RAINBOW/ PUSH Coalition. "If my mind can conceive it, and my heart can believe it, I know I can achieve it."

Barack Obama.

44th and first African American President of the United States of America. "Yes, we can."

Andrew Young.

African American Civil Rights leader, diplomat and Pastor: "Wishing, of all strategies, is the worst. Rosa Parks was the inspiration . . . simply by the act of her being who she was, a sweet and loving and simple child of God who refused to let anybody or anything force her to compromise her spirit."

Africa Fact

In the 19th century European colonizers drew an "International Treaty" by which they partitioned Africa, each marking their area of possession of both the people and their heritage. The partitioning disregarded the ethnic, social and economic composition of local people. This has been the cause of endless years of liberation wars and ethnic conflicts as Africans fought for their independence.

African voices continue to speak to the generations of Africa

Dedan Kimathi, 1920-1957
Martyred leader of the Kenyan Land and Freedom Army who heroically organised Kenyans to fight British colonial settlers after they declared Kenya a protectorate and forcibly moved Kenyans from their lands and turned them into forced **labour,** *"Let's seek freedom together for our people."*

Chapter 7

The beauty of African-ness. Black people must begin to promote the integrity of African-ness by expressing it in things such as culture, dress and food.

7 African Patriots

*T*rain up a child in the way he should go and when he grows up he will not *depart from it*

King Solomon

*Y*ou probably know that Solomon was the Jewish king who gained the reputation of being the wisest man in the world. Reading through some of his sayings in the book of Proverbs, it is not hard to understand why he gained this reputation. He and his father David are held in extremely high esteem, even revered by their own Jewish nation as well as by history and by billions of people all over the world.

No doubt when Solomon asserted that the childhood training of a child determines the future course of his life, aspirations and behaviour, he was reminiscing on how the ways his father and mother had trained him had impacted the course of his own life, aspirations and achievements. Not least, Solomon was a shrewd political leader who built on the foundation of his father's achievements and led his nation into a period of outstanding prosperity and influence.

One of the statements recorded in the Psalms of David, Solomon's father, reads, "*If I forget you, Jerusalem, let my right hand stop working, if I do not exalt you above my chief joy, let my tongue cleave to the roof of my mouth*". It is clear that both by words and deeds, David trained his son Solomon into the passionate patriotism—love for his country, people and nation—that fuelled his wise leadership of his nation.

When I interact with Black people around the world, one of the heart-breaking themes I hear in their words and observe in their deeds is a pervasive self-hate and a lack of patriotism which in some cases has grown into an outright dislike of blackness, African-ness and of the Continent and countries of Africa. In some cases, it is a case of being ashamed of their Land and People. I have met Black people who will not tell you what country they come from—or will lie about it for sheer embarrassment with their roots. Clearly, there is, among Black people, a crisis of patriotism.

I do understand that many Black nations are in a state of poverty, deprivation and sometimes violence and political confusion—and often Black leaders and people are themselves to blame. Millions of Black people are in diaspora, especially in Western nations, as economic refugees seeking a better life. Many have opted to assimilate in these far off lands and to do their best to forget Africa as a bad dream. Their children, born in the Diaspora, have no idea of their identity and their parents feel it would be a great elevation if these children could become, say, as European as possible. It is a generation which will, not by the slave trade, but by parental default through ignorance and inferiority suffer the perpetual trauma of loss of identity and self-esteem.

Black people need to urgently wake up to the fact that many of the nations in favour of which they are abandoning Africa used to be in just as needy a state, if not worse, than Africa is. They were developed into the state they are chiefly by one resource—the love and commitment of their own people to their own country—the patriotism of their people. Even nations like the United States of America went through such hardships as civil wars and times of deep poverty such as the great depression of the 1930's. But because of their love and commitment to their own land, it did not occur to these people to abandon their country. They stayed, fought and worked until they built their country into a state of competitiveness, all the time teaching their children at every turn that there is no better nation to belong to than theirs.

Black people everywhere—in Africa, in America, in the Indies, Europe and other places, need to work seriously to restore this resource—patriotism—the passionate love of Blackness, Africa and African-ness, particularly into the hearts and minds of the children and youth. When it is re-discovered, African-ness will be found to be a priceless asset, not only to Black people, but to the whole world. But to be re-discovered, African-ness must be first embraced by its divinely appointed stewards—Black people everywhere. The young Black people must hear this passionate message from their parents, *'If I forget thee o Africa, let my right hand stop working, if I do not promote you above my chief joy, let my tongue cleave to the roof of my mouth.'*

The generation of Black leaders, both on the African continent and abroad, whose dreams birthed the present improvement of the lot of Black people, possessed a great love and commitment to Africa. Great African—American leaders such as Dr Martin Luther King Jr networked with leaders in Africa for mutual inspiration. You only need to read a few pages of the writings of Marcus Garvey to see that he carried in his heart a fierce love and commitment to African-ness. Malcolm X and other Black leaders in America went on journeys of pilgrimage back to Africa and inspired other Black people to do so.

This love and commitment to Africa on the part of African Americans must be revived as parents teach their children the true value of their irreplaceable roots and a new generation of African American youth begin to travel to Africa and to join hands with African youth to strengthen African-ness to mutual benefit.

On the continent of Africa itself, political leaders must not abandon the concept of African-ness which was espoused by all the founding fathers. If a love and commitment to Africa is not built up in the hearts of African youth, even relatively developed African nations will continue to see an exodus of their young people who are being relentlessly trained by an untiring Western media machine to love and admire the West and to despise their own continent. The brain drain will continue and accelerate.

One statistician told me that there are more Malawian doctors in the English city of Manchester than in the whole nation of Malawi. The demon of Afrophobia needs to be exorcised from the hearts of Black people. When Black people learn to love Africa, they will follow their hearts to the continent and rapidly develop it.

Although the task of rebuilding love and commitment to Africa and to African-ness looks formidable, it is in truth quite achievable, provided we understand two simple issues. First, in what things is the love of African-ness constituted? Second, who is best placed to build in the heart of the child and the young person that love and commitment?

Patriotism—love and commitment—is constituted in an attachment and love to such simple things as *a way of life*. What you eat, what you wear, culture, language, the morals you value, ways of relating to people around you, entertainment and other simple things form a love, commitment and attachment. If you take a good look at Black people, nothing, from food, dress, entertainment and ways of behaviour—almost nothing—is rooted in or inspired by African-ness. In fact, the African things are despised by Africans, regardless of whether they are better, more relevant or wholesome than alien things. Almost everything is adopted from other peoples.

African culture and morals would certainly have protected Black people from scourges such as HIV and disintegrating families. African traditional foods are healthier and far more nutritious than Western foods. African robes are more comfortable, colourful and better fitted to climate. The African community is more supportive and inclusive. African entertainment is not designed to damage morals, but to build wholesome personalities.

Secondly, it is parents who are best placed to foster attachment and love to these things in their children. Last month, I went through the pain of bidding farewell to my father. Apinos Wutawunashe—1924-2011: we buried him under a shady grove at the family estate after he completed nearly eighty-seven years of a life lived fully and fruitfully, as a proud African, in Africa. When I look at the things and way of life I love or am attached to, I see his fingerprints all over them, particularly in the season of my childhood. My favourite foods are the village foods he loved—from the peanut butter pumpkin and bean pulp to the dried summer greens.

The African folk stories I listened to him telling to gatherings of school children through word and song when he was a schools superintendent not only ring in my memory, but have influenced my life with their wisdom and morals. The long drives he took me through the incomparably beautiful African countryside, sometimes taking me on hill climbs from the summits of which we would just gaze in wonder at the countryside, taught me to love the hills, rivers and lakes of Africa. He would teach me African bush—craft and point out to me wild fruits and medicinal plants. He would often take me deep in the villages and sit with me in the company of old African rural folk who would tell us the names of little hills and streams and the history of our progenitors. It gave me a strong sense of my identity to pass on to my children. I cannot forget the way he never allowed me to mix English words with the words of my African mother tongue, and helped me take pride in speaking my own language.

Then he would teach me and my siblings the words of praise with which people of my totem would be thanked and appreciated when they accomplished something good or brought back a good kill from the hunt.

I am forever grateful that my parents exposed us to the hard manual work and rural rhythm of the African village. It left me with an ethic of community, hard work and responsibility. They referred me to my aunts and uncles to teach me responsible habits as I grew into my teenage years. They trained me and my siblings to fear God, to honour any and every older person and to always receive and care for people. They would frequently tell us how important Black People are, and lecture us on the justness of the cause of the leaders who were mobilising for the fight for equity for Black people. All this left in me a deep and undying love, attachment and commitment to Africa.

It is parents—you the father, the mother, who are best placed to build love and commitment to Africa in your children. How? By training them to love the simple things of the African way of life. Deliberately change the foods you serve in your home to reflect a heavy bias towards African foods. Train them in the simple respectful manners as well as in the wholesome morals of the African culture. Take them to the African village and countryside from time to time and teach them to bond with the soil, the cows, the chickens and the goats—and of course, the grandparents and extended family. Teach them what you know—the stories, the games, their identity and history. Deliberately require them to speak their mother language fluently. Affirm African-ness to them and teach them to love telling people of other colours who they are and where they come from. Begin to include items of dress that reflect African-ness in your and their wardrobe. Do not leave them at the mercy of the Western media mammoth, but train them to discern decent things from indecent, and to challenge agendas and editorial lines that falsely elevate politicians and people of other colours above Black people. Create in them zeal to learn about Black people. *Train up the children in the way they should go.*

Black children born in the Diaspora, or taken there at an early age are especially vulnerable to the evil of having their African identity, culture, language and ways of life completely vacuumed out of them. The responsibility for this atrocity lies ironically on the shoulders of apathetic parents. Or parents who suffer from the misconception that embracing the western way of life and values is a form of cultural ascendance. I recently visited a church in one of the European countries which has Africans as the bulk of its membership. The Black Pastor told me how they had decided to initiate in the congregation a program that would enhance African-ness in the congregation and particularly in the children. As part of the program they take twenty minutes after every service to teach from the pulpit the four main African languages represented in the church. After this they serve a lunch made up of African dishes from various areas of the continent. He excitedly told me how this simple program had boosted the confidence of the Black children in the church within this society in which they are a minority.

In the home and in any other useful forum Black parents in the Diaspora need to take deliberate steps to train up their children in African-ness, African languages and ways. These young people will grow up with a love and attachment to Africa, love which is the basis for patriotism.

There are, of course, other Africans—for example those displaced into western nations through the slave trade—who do not have an idea of where they came from, their language or the way of life. For most of these Black people, an assimilation born out of despair is the choice they are forced to make. However it was heartening to see Black people, for example in America during the latter half of the twentieth century, insist that they be referred to as Africans (hence the emergence of the appellation "African-American").

In some religious circles there are also impressive programs to enhance African-ness among African Americans. This is as it should be and Black people all over the world must network and initiate focused projects and modules which will help African Americans and other Black people to learn about the Continent, its ways of life and even some major languages, so that African-ness may once again be expressed by those from whom it was violently snatched.

There must certainly rise up a love for Africa and a patriotism that will cause many Black People in the Diaspora to return to the Continent and build it up. This latter day Exodus is sure to come as an African consciousness gains momentum.

I am, of course, obliged to acknowledge that it might not be realistic to expect every Black person to return to Africa. The global village is an abiding reality, but Black people must fight to express African-ness and a love for it in every nation on the Earth where they happen to be. The Jews for example, scattered as they are as citizens of the many nations of the world, clearly manifest a Jewish patriotism-a love and commitment to their identity and motherland akin to that of David and Solomon. So too do some other nationalities.

The season has come for the aggressive rise of an African International patriotism, which will gain in momentum as we Black people learn to train up our youth and children in the way they should go-*the way of African-ness.*

African voices continue to speak to the generations of Africa

Walter Sisulu, *1912-2003*
A leading anti apartheid activist and co-founding member of the African National Congress who built the organization into an organized, massive Liberation Movement, "When I took up the position of being a secretary-general, that very night I knew, finished with me: I can't go to business, I can't be employed, I've got a duty to the people."

Chapter 8

Tommie Smith and John Carlos

After winning the gold and bronze medals in the 1968 Olympics, Tommie Smith and John Carlos used their success and visibility to protest against the plight of Black people from the Holocaust to the resultant present day poverty. They raised their fists in the Black Power salute. Black people who attain success in any field, must use that platform to speak out and carry on the struggle of disadvantaged Black people.

8   The New Leader

*A*sk not what your country can do for you, but what you can do for your country.

President John Fitzgerald Kennedy

*T*hese simple yet deeply profound words were spoken by John F. Kennedy in his inauguration speech as he ascended to the presidency of the United States of America as perhaps the most popular president that nation ever had. And I am persuaded that in a nutshell he summarised the sense of mission with which those who want to answer the high calling of political leadership of Black people should approach this calling with.

Time and again, there rises among a people a political leader who makes an indelible mark on the hearts of his people and even on the hearts of people all over the world. These leaders always seem to make history, yet for some reason most of them end up getting shot or assassinated in some painful way or another. I suppose this highlights a never ending battle between good and evil, light and darkness.

I am always thankful and genuinely awed by individuals whom I see aspiring to become political leaders, particularly political leaders of African people. The political arena is by no means a comfort zone. As I watch the news casts it often seems to me that those who ascend to political leadership have to endure daily insults and criticism from the very people they are trying to serve. And then of course you need eyes even in the back of your head because it is not only the opposition which is trying to pull you down, but even those on your side are hawkishly watching for the opportunity to find fault in you and replace you. Yet another occupational hazard of African politics is the ever present threat of violence or death. Because democracy was never allowed an African evolution, politicians on opposite sides often tend to regard each other as mortal enemies rather than as healthy competitors offering to serve people.

Then there is the ever humiliating pontificating of powerful nations, mostly former colonial masters who for some reason seem to be continually able, no matter what recent massacre their own leaders have been responsible for, to turn the moral tables against Black leaders, in spite of how much smaller the scope of the latter's offences may have been in comparison with theirs. As a matter of fact, these powers maintain and finance a special court particularly focussed on the misdeeds, perceived or otherwise, chiefly of African leaders, before which their own leaders are guaranteed never to appear. I do not know what kind of modern witch's spell has been administered on African political leaders to quietly acquiesce to this schoolmaster-schoolboy relationship. It is heartening though of late to hear Black leaders assert that African leaders who err should face an African justice in Africa.

Another gauntlet which African political leaders run is the endemic poverty of their nations, the foundations of which were dug very deep by former colonial and slave masters. Despite never having offered Africa a Marshall plan after four centuries of plundering them, these world powers expect Africa to compete on the world economic stage, and do not hesitate when it suits them to use this poverty to incite entire African populations against their political leaders. Watching that mighty giant which is the international press, and reading the releases of international anti-corruption watchdogs, it often puzzles me why a half million dollar bribe received by a corrupt African leader is always portrayed as being so massively more sinister than a billion dollar bribe paid by some powerful Western government to some oil rich bozo to encourage him to loot the treasury and buy armaments from them.

I often wish I could find a platform from which to tell Black people that their political leaders are no worse, and in many cases stand on much higher moral ground than the leaders of powerful nations who are standing in judgement over them. It is important to understand this lest many heroic Black leaders be condemned to historical waste heaps to which these former masters have never consigned even the worst of their own leaders.

First, it is important to appreciate deeply the generation of Black and African political leaders, many of whom are still alive, who navigated the perilous waters of a world which sought only to degrade and plunder Black people, and led their people, at great personal cost, to political liberation. Black people must never forget these leaders, nor should they ever take their sacrifices for granted. It is important to tell the exploits and achievements of these heroes to children and youth in every generation. I agree that these heroes have in many cases not been perfect, but it impoverishes a people when they discard their own heroes on the basis of idealistic standards to which no one on earth has ever attained. It is also a fact of life that criticism of leaders is often deeply flawed and all too often guided by the motivated vitriol of political rivalry.

Yet this call for Black people to value their own leaders places an even heavier responsibility on the shoulders of Black political leaders to fight for ever higher moral ground. Indeed, no one should ever aspire for the leadership of Black people with a heart that is asking what they can do for him or her. This has been the plight of Black people—that those who reigned over them in the past tragic years of subjugation came asking only the question, "What can these Black people do for me, what can I take from them?"

Black people have built with their unremunerated sweat and broken backs nations and empires for other peoples who are now regarded as super powers and as the developed world. Even their children and loved ones were snatched from them by colonial tyranny and slave trade. Barely decades after the last of these untried crimes were committed, Black people find themselves gazing longingly, even enviously, at wealth plundered from them that adorns the palaces and courts of the potentates of other peoples. Their hearts are yearning for the kind of leader who will come asking in his or her heart, "What can I do for my people, what can I give to them, how can I serve them—how can I lift up these beautiful abused Black people?"

For all who seek to lead or are in political leadership of Black people, there is an awesome array of past mentors whose travails spoke of men and women who sought to answer the question, "What can I do for my people?" There is the martyrs' roll—the men and women who hold up their heads from eternity and say to all Black people, "I gave you my very life that you may be free and stand in your place of dignity."

Legends like Dr Martin Luther King Jr: for his Dream for Black people, they shot him in Memphis, Tennessee. Giants like Malcolm X—for his empowering ideology they sponsored traitors to slay him with impunity. The dynamic and incomparable Patrice Lumumba of Congo—for his dangerous theme of uniting all the Congo's tribes his murder was sanctioned in Western capitals. The visionary Bantu Steven Biko: for fighting to restore to the Black man his identity, dignity, self-confidence and self-reliance they tortured him to death in an Apartheid dungeon. Indeed, every free Black nation has an impressive martyrs' roll, including children massacred for protesting.

Then there are those who endured literally decades in prisons, those who suffered unspeakable acts of torture and harassment. Like the simply great Nelson Mandela, whom they condemned to the harsh Robben Island for years on the grounds that he was a subversive. He came out and shocked everyone by building an inclusive democracy based on reconciliation, in much the same way as Zimbabwe's Patriotic Front, led by Mugabe and Nkomo, had done before him. Most African leaders came out of years of imprisonment to lead their people to freedom—Jomo Kenyatta, Hastings Kamuzu Banda, Robert Mugabe, Joshua Nkomo and many others throughout Southern, East, Central and West Africa. Then there are the battle and exile leaders, such as Oliver Tambo, Sam Nujoma and others, who endured incredible dangers of war and deprivation. With respect, John F Kennedy did not have half the comprehension these Africans had of the personal sacrifice he called for when he said, "Ask not what your country can do for you, but what you can do for your country".

Then there is the unique heart of Black people themselves. If there is a people who deserve to be led with a heart that seeks to serve them and to restore all the dignity they were robbed of, it is the Black people. The African people know how to give all their heart, mind, body and soul to a leader. They will follow a leader with a heart-warming loyalty that even puzzles other peoples. This is why it is the more puzzling that for some Black political leaders, the choice tool with which to lead their people is fear. Where does the heart come from that does not hesitate to incite the masses of Black people to beat and kill each other for political ends? Dear African leader, give to your people the gift of peace. The slave master flogged them, the colonial master shot and tortured them. To you their fellow Black leader they cry, *"Restore our dignity and our humanness! Give us rest, give us peace at last!"*

One of the major issues which African political leaders, indeed African governments, must confront and re-address urgently is the issue of Western democracy. Recently I watched with sadness as an African leader in a country where a violent election had led to a stalemate said angrily, *"How can I share power . . . ."* As he spoke like that, the body toll was rising as his and his rival's supporters slaughtered each other on the street. It immediately dawned on me that there are two key words which are the root of Africans 'chronic problems with the Western model of democracy. Western democracy is deeply rooted in the concept of **competition** for **power**. In other words, let my people give me power. I will compete for it at any cost.

And so, periodically, in order to satisfy the expectations mainly of former colonial masters whose systems of governance Africans are imitating without thinking of their relevance to their people, African politicians subject their people to a violent, murderous and definitely un African season of vicious competition for power, culminating in elections which sometimes end in civil wars. One of the pictures I am failing to delete from my mind is that of a Black man running in an East African capital with an arrow that had been shot through his head by supporters of a rival political party because their respective leaders could not agree on the results of an election. Hundreds of men, women and children died in a matter of days. Actually, this is not democracy. Even prides of lions in the jungle have wiser and less costly ways of determining leadership. Yet African leaders have tacitly accepted that the slaughter is an acceptable price for practising Western democracy and getting nods of approval from their former masters.

I submit to our leaders and to the world that there is nothing intrinsically wrong with Africans when it comes to democracy. The problem is that, just like in other areas of life, out of an inferiority complex fostered by years of subjugation, African political leaders are thoughtlessly adopting a former master's type of democracy instead of having the courage and wisdom to design their own democracy, suited to their people in the spirit of self-determination. A three piece woollen suit was designed for near zero temperatures in a Westminster chamber of Parliament. African politicians will make this suit official dress in a thirty-five degree temperature chamber in a tropical African city. They feel there is something inferior about cool African garments. The judges' wigs are even more bizarre, especially the blond ones being designed for Black lady judges. No one even notices that Western democracy was still called democracy when Black people were not even allowed to vote!

A brief look at history will illustrate that Western democracy evolved or was crafted literally through centuries in which its momentum did not only take into account the vote, but also the economic and social welfare and rights of people in nations which had to overcome such systems as the semi-slavery of feudalism and serfdom. Former institutions such as the monarchy for example were negotiated into forms that would suit the culture and the people. Freedoms and rights in the context of the people's needs were progressively agreed upon. When the society had dealt with fundamental issues of access to bread and butter it then in modern times continued its debate to such controversial 'delicacies' as legislating the rights of men to marry men and carry government paper to that effect, though they might find it difficult to legislate male pregnancies.

My intention here is not to enter the sexual rights debate, on which I have clear views, but rather to ask, should African nations which have not yet found answers to issues of giving their people rights to be free from poverty and to leave squatter settlements be imitating developed nations who can feed every unemployed person, in spending millions on legislation that men should marry men, just in order to gain the approval of the West? I read somewhere that the city of Constantinople was overrun by enemies while ecclesiastical elders who were in charge of the city's defences were locked in debate on the subject "if a fly falls into holy water, what happens: does the fly become holy or the water contaminated?"

Seriously, if other nations panel-beat their own democracies to become relevant to the ethos of their people, so should Africans. Black political leaders need to sit down and craft a democracy and system of governance that takes into account such critically relevant issues as poverty, tribal and other diversity issues, the culture and way of life of their people, and so on. The British, for example, accommodated their tribal problem by creating tribal parliaments with agreed powers—Welsh, Scottish, Irish even. An African man wants to raise his head in the council and see his tribe fairly represented, not just a house filled with the cleverest people in the country.

One of the solutions to senseless and bloody political competitions based on dog-eat-dog is to recognise that the deepest theme of African culture is consensus. There can be a democracy based on consensus, and not competition. It may not be necessary to change leaders every three years. We may need a council made up of delegates from various tribes—and so on. The issues that cause violence, retribution and refusals to give up power are often based on systems that are in discord with national needs.

I trust we have all noticed how the Chinese are overtaking everyone economically. A major key to their success is that their kind of democracy brings them all to the place where everyone pursues the same objective. They do not have a discordant society. They analysed the psyche of their people and based their system on this kind of consensus. No one clapped for them in approval, but they had the courage to adopt a system born out of themselves and attuned to the character of their people. Now nations who criticised them are borrowing money from them, and, significantly, are mealy-mouthed when it comes to political commentary on the Chinese.

I put the case that in its present economic state, Africa needs to craft a democratic system based on a consensus which will help them to focus energy on building their economies rather than on burning energy every few years on electoral tribal wars. An African democracy must be heavily weighted towards securing economic and welfare rights for its people. It must also be focussed on raising the ideological, political, educational and social awareness of its people so that they can genuinely participate in the nation's affairs. Having freedom to vote in a nation where you have no idea what is going on is not democracy, no matter how long voting queues are, or what big nation approves of it.

One of Africa's heart-warming stories is the story of the nation of Botswana. Its wise old Lion King Seretse Khama avoided colonisation by negotiating a protectorate from which emerged a peaceful and free democratic nation in which governments have smoothly changed through the vote. The current President of Botswana is a remarkable and relatively young descendant of the old Lion King, and answers to a name heavily weighted with African royal legacy—President Lieutenant—General Seretse Khama Ian Khama. Visiting this beautiful nation, I have often seen Ian Khama, often with cabinet ministers in tow, sitting at large village fireside gatherings of his people, listening to their concerns, answering their questions and explaining to them in terms they can understand the resources which the nation and government can make available to them. I believe this African Prince is demonstrating an essential ingredient which must be added to African democracy to make it meaningful—bringing the issues down to the level where the common people can understand them and thus act as informed judges when they vote. There are approved 'democracies' on the Continent where the truth is that people are voting blindfolded—with literally not a clue about what they are voting for or about.

African democracy has not yet emerged. It must be designed, crafted and owned by Africans themselves. Because of inappropriate political systems, most African politicians find it hard to focus on *doing what needs to be done for their people.* The system forces them to focus on political survival, and more often than not, even on physical survival. This warped focus in turn breeds a paranoid politician who is asking not what he can do for his people, but rather what his people can be used or abused to do for him in the uncertain period of tenure available to him.

The courage, wisdom and initiative to craft an African democracy is urgent. Nations which have designed their own political systems, and not just duck-taped or copied and pasted concepts on a template designed by former colonial masters, will end up with a presence of strength and integrity in the community of nations. If Africa's political leaders desire this position which holds the promise of advantage to their people, it is now time to roll up their sleeves and design an *African Democracy.* The season of the politics and democracy of a schoolboy under a colonial schoolmaster needs to come to an end in Africa. It must give way to a democracy designed, and therefore owned, by Black people—an African Democracy. Among other things, an African Democracy is sure to be more humane than the individualistic systems that surround and seek to suffocate us.

Above all, an African Democracy will provide an enabling environment for an army of political leaders who are waiting to serve Black people through a system they can own and identify with—an African system. With their deeds of service to their people they will continually declare:

> *"Ask not what your people can do for you, but what you can do for your people."*

African voices continue to speak to the generations of Africa

Lobengula, 1845-1894.
Last Ndebele King (Zimbabwe) who fought British Settlers over the minerals of his land.

Chapter 9

A lone voice for justice

This inspired man is symbolic of all non-Black People who fought for freedom and justice on the side of Black People.

9 Dear Africa,

*D*ear Africa,

Andrew Wutawunashe

I woke up this morning in a deeply reflective mood and I decided to write this letter to you, sharing with you the burdens of my heart.

It is to you that I write, for you are my people, my natural family-I am a part of you—you are close to my heart. I am, because you are. Indeed I am together with you, for as my fathers would say, a person is a person through others—Umuntu ngumuntu ngabantu. Your poverty, your pain, your humiliation, is my distress. Your prosperity, your peace and your dignity is my exaltation. Your division and weakness is my undoing. Your unity and strength is my making, my livelihood.

Dear Africa, you are not just a line encircling a piece of land on the world map. You are every Black man, woman and child on the face of the earth who originated from this Continent. You are the Jamaican, the Haitian, the West Indian, the Black

Brazilian and the African American. Some of us may not live on your ground, but you live eternally in our hearts, in our minds, in our blood and in our veins.

The laughter of the Black children in Atlanta, in Kingston, in London, in Amsterdam, in Paris, in Sao Paulo, in Accra, in Lagos, in Nairobi, in Harare and Johannesburg, is the laughter of African children. The blood of Black youth gunned down by crime in the Bronx, in Moss Side, in Kinshasa, in Port au Prince, in Mogadishu or in Alexandra is the blood of African youth. Poverty, humiliation and discrimination against Black people on every continent is the abuse of African people. The triumph of Black leaders, clergy, entrepreneurs and sports people in the world's arenas is the triumph of African people. The pulse and melody of your artists on the world's screens, stages and galleries is the dynamic of African people.

I asked who I am today and I heard Thabo Mbeki from his podium for African Liberation and Renaissance say, "I am an African". That is why I write to you today, Africa, wherever you are, and say to you, "It is time to pause and reflect." With reflection must come burden, with burden must come thought and strategizing and after this must come action-for none can change our situation but ourselves. And none of us is too small to do something.

You are an exciting colour on the beautiful tapestry of the different families which God Almighty painted as His creation on the canvas of the Earth. He wanted you to stand out, possess your portion and in dignity make your contribution that would enrich the families of the earth. Yet in so many ways you were plundered and brought down by the cunning, greed and violence of some races on the face of the earth. I say to you today, God's plan must not be aborted. You must at last rise up, take your place, take your portion and make your contribution to the families of the Earth.

Dear Africa, be courageous and take a good look at your face today. This earth was designed to be a place of competition. You will get what you think you deserve. You *will become what you think you are worth. You will achieve what you are willing to fight for. Look at your face. It is like you have accepted the place of weakness, the place of dependence, the place of division. It is like you have adopted the fractures which the cunning divided you with so that you may never be strong. It's like you have accepted the place to be forever the imitator of other peoples and of consuming only what others make. It seems you think your continent is not worth staying in, fighting its problems and developing it. You have lost your love for your own land. You can't see that others with lands that have been devastated are developing them and overtaking you.*

Dear Africa, it is time to rise up and build yourself up to a place of strength among the nations. Look back and remember the dreams of those who started the struggles for your freedom and restoration—from Harriet Tubman to Martin Luther King Jr.; from Kwame Nkrumah to Nelson Mandela. Remember the dreams of those who shed their blood for you, from Patrice Lumumba to Bantu Steven Biko to the Unknown Soldier who fell in the bitter struggles for your freedom and dignity. They all dreamed that you would restore your identity and undo the mental shackles and all the damage that had been inflicted on you. They dreamed that your leaders and people would fight fiercely to heal the fractures, to unite you, to build one Africa. One Africa, a place of Black strength, politically, socially, economically and militarily.

Do not betray these dreams. Do not abort them. For those who do not fight for their identity, for their dignity, for their unity and for their competitiveness will one day soon find themselves slaves once again.

You the leaders, you that have risen to the places where you can be heard by the world, do not be flattered into abandoning the struggle of the Black people. Seek not to please the rich and powerful nations of this world for they fight first for their own advantage. For the sake of Africa, let your ideas spring up and let your voices once again be heard.

Dear Africa, rise up, for the future lot of your youth and children depends on the path you now take. Your people may be silent, but they have strong dreams and there are fires of hope in their hearts. They look on with expectation that leaders will arise and take them to their Promised Land. Why do you sleep? Arise, build yourself up and fight for yourself, dear Africa. It is time!

With a strong hope with a passionate prayer I remain

One of your beloved sons,
Andrew Wutawunashe.

Some Of Africa's Heroes, Visionaries And Liberators speak

Bingu wa Mutharika
African economist, passionate Pan Africanist and current President of Malawi. He authored several books on Africa including One Africa One Destiny, "... the best way to attain African renaissance is to free the African mindset from colonial and neo-colonial indoctrination."

Chapter 10

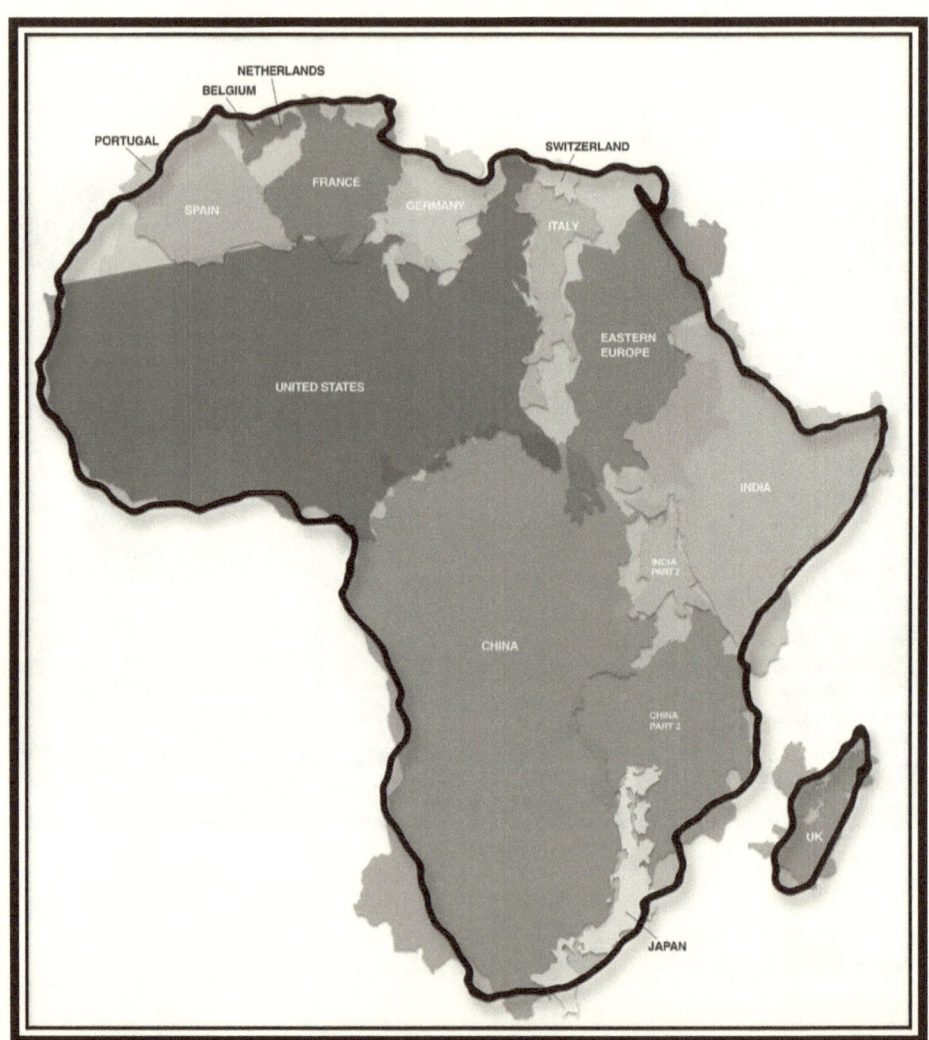

How big is Africa?

China, India, USA, Europe and Alaska together are smaller in area than Africa. Black people must believe in the potential of Africa to one day lead and feed the world.

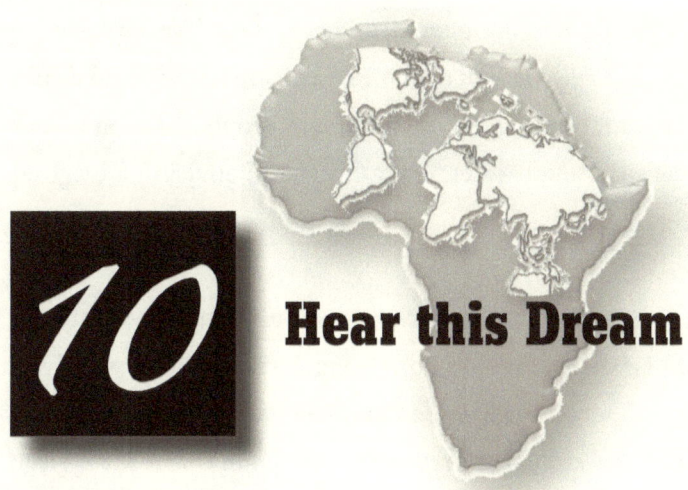

10 **Hear this Dream**

*H*ear this dream which I have dreamed . . . your sheaves stood round about, and made obeisance to my sheaf . . . ,"

Young Joseph

*F*ew writers, if any, have ever captured the sheer intensity of the groaning of Black People during the years of their subjugation and suffering under colonialism and apartheid as did that great writer, Alan Paton.

His book, *Cry, the Beloved Country*, set as an English literature text book in my early years in African junior high school, left an indelible sense of the painful sighs of Africa occasioned by the social conditions of the poverty that spawned a culture of crime among young Black people living in an atmosphere of endemic fear.

That haunting, mournful yet poetic refrain lingers powerfully in the mind of any who had the privilege of reading the story: "*. . . Cry the beloved country; cry* *for the unborn child that is the inheritor of our fear. Let him not love the earth too deeply; nor laugh . . . for fear will rob him of all this."* You are left with no doubt that these were the lamentations of a compassionate prophet during a dark season in which it was so difficult to embrace hope and envision a brighter future for Black People.

Yet if Paton could read this book today, because I simply cannot recreate the awesome emotion of his words, I would put an aggressive positive parody to his words and rather say, *"Dream, the Beloved Continent; dream for the sake of the unborn Black child that he inherit not our reproach. Teach him to love the African continent very deeply-to be moved when the birds of his land are singing—to give all his heart to its mountains and valleys . . . for it is God's endowment to him for his greatness and competitiveness among the nations."*

In this generation, we owe past, present and future generations of Black People a debt of something that is intriguing in its simplicity, and yet so baffling in its elusiveness. No people, no nation has ever risen to a place of greatness and competitiveness on the face of the earth without this simple thing. Those who found and nurtured it as a people overcame great odds and built themselves to places of great achievement on the face of the earth. Those who found it, under estimated it and abandoned it aborted great things that would have surely come. Those who didn't find it never really aspired to much.

What is this great thing, this great key, that we owe Black People everywhere? It is not money or wealth—but it will create great wealth. Misreading the game, Black People are crying out for aid from rich nations, or taking great pains to abandon the African Continent to go and enjoy the finished fruits of far off lands—oblivious to the fact that it is this key that inspired the peoples of those nations to build themselves into conditions of stability, wealth and competitiveness.

Whenever I see all those Africans risking their lives to cross seas in small boats so that they may live in Europe or some other nations as economic refugees, I am reminded of that great story—parable—*Acres of Diamonds.* In the story, a poor farmer, struggling on his land through which runs a stream, to make his fortune, hears of a legendary place reputed to have acres of diamonds to be picked off the ground. The poor farmer leaves his land to go and find his fortune in these acres of diamonds. After decades of quest, now a sick dying old man, he decides to give up his quest and return to his farm to die. A few days after getting back home, he hobbles to the stream on his land. When he bends down to touch the water, he sees diamonds in the shallow water, on the stream bank—and yes—everywhere. Only then does he realise that the legendary land with acres of diamonds has always actually been his own farm!

I wonder why Africans seem to be the only people not to wake up to the fact that the world's number one destination for wealth and resources is actually Africa! The answer to this blind misdirection is this key we owe our generations.

So what is this all important key, you may ask? It is a key within the reach of every Black person, and even children, should I say, more so children—are able to grasp this key.

This is the key. We owe Black People **a Dream—an African Dream.** Yes, a dream—for it is the abstract substance of a dream that is the foundation upon which great and competitive nations are built.

To date, Americans speak clearly of the American Dream, and time and again refer to the 'pursuit of happiness' to which they were inspired centuries ago by their founding fathers who were mere religious refugees. The British near conquered the world on the sail of the twin dream of greatness and empire—calling their tiny island Great Britain. Through the socialist dream great nations like China and the Soviet Union were built.

Africa's biggest problem is *there is no African Dream*. The season that birthed great progress among Africans and Black People everywhere was the season of the Dreamers. Dr Martin Luther King Junior galvanised Black People into protests and activism that led to the official desegregation of the United States of America with the historic words, *'I have a dream . . .'* The legacy of dreamers of the ascent of Black People, like Marcus Garvey and others, is evident everywhere among Black People. Then an army of dreamers of African Liberation and Unity, such as Kwame Nkrumah and others rose up and birthed the decolonised Africa we know today.

As the season of liberation ran its course, Black People made a serious blunder: they stopped dreaming, and worse still, abandoned the dreams of their Founding Fathers. The problem could well be that Black People only saw things in the reactionary mode of solving colonial problems. So, instead of identifying visions and dreams, they simply looked at new Black governments as vehicles for solving past problems and 'delivering services' to them. They did not necessarily see themselves as bearing the responsibility of building up the Promised Land. I have visited Black countries where in certain cities the last buildings were constructed during colonial times, scores of years past.

Whatever the reason, the tragic result is that the Black Person is left without the most important key to creativeness, competitiveness and greatness. He has been left without a dream. It is therefore critical that an African Dream be defined, taught and endeared to every Black man, woman, boy, girl and child.

Every existing Pan African organ, such as the African Union and Regional Organs should make the enunciation of the African Dream their first priority.

Every school, educational and training institution should devote time to daily write this dream in the hearts and minds of Africans, young and old. The Media and the arts should birth lyrics, poems, and movies, theatrical and other productions to endear the Dream to Africans everywhere. Governments should assign and empower departments to educate and win hearts to the African Dream. *There should be an Africa we dream about.*

Simplistic as all this may sound, it is the most powerful principle for mobilising the commitment, passion and creativity which Africa needs in order to ascend. Black People have for some reason substituted the need to have and pursue their own Dream with a childish and short sighted consumerism which sees them everywhere abandoning their own creativity in favour of consuming things made by other peoples. A culture of this nature will, if adhered to, ensure that Africa will never become a competitive continent.

Africa must learn, like other nations that have become competitive, to re-invent all sorts of wheels and put an African brand on them. Competitiveness does not always call for originality. The Americans shamelessly recruited former Nazis to help them make advanced weaponry and even advanced their space program with Hitler's technology. The Soviets did not hesitate to do the same. Dr Mahathir Mohammed inspired the people of Malaysia with a dream to transform Malaysia into a modern competitive nation with a cunning mixture of re-invented wheels, like the Malaysian car, and by attracting Silicon Valley to come and manufacture micro-chips with cheaper and more relaxed labour conditions in his country—all the time using the opportunity to acquire advanced technology for Malaysia.

In the Africa of dreamers, African vehicles will ply the roads; skyscrapers with distinctly African architectural themes will adorn the skyline. The Shaka fighter aircraft will be assembled by a Pan-African consortium. The Nkrumah

Space Station will be manned by scientists from all over Africa. Indigenous technologies will enhance the comfort and productivity of African villages.

When there is an African Dream, it will inspire numerous dreams in the hearts and minds of individual Africans, and they will enterprise for African competitiveness in every field.

These simple components are needed in order to constitute the African Dream. First there must be a spiritual component—**the Dream must embody a passionate love for Africa and a deep commitment to her.** Part of the Jew's dream for Jerusalem is, 'If *I forget thee oh Jerusalem, may my right hand lose its cunning'*. Let us bring Paton to fullness and say *'Let us love Africa very deeply.'*

Africa is a continent that has always warmed the hearts of all that came to its beautiful shores. Foreigners have loved Africa to the place of insisting they be buried there. Ironically, it is the Black Person, the African whose heart is now cold towards the Land of his divine endowment. This lack of love and commitment causes Africans to abandon the continent and suffer humiliation as minorities in far off lands. It's a wicked deception!

Dear Africa; it's time to love Africa once more, and to teach your children that there is no better land on the face of the earth than Africa. There is no better being than the essence of African-ness. I have heard people ask 'How can we love this continent with its poverty, wars and political pressures?'

Love for Africa is the fuel that will cause us to stay and solve the problems of the continent. It was because of love for their land that Americans did not run anywhere during the years of the Great Depression, but stayed, kept on dreaming, worked hard and transformed it. It is those who love it who will change the painful face of Africa. A new love for Africa must rise again until we can say with real passion and sincerity and the words of one great African dreamer and Liberator,

"I am an African . . ."

Love for Africa must also embody in it a love for People and things African. This is why again the Black Person must express Africa in even such simple things as dress and food, and in practising and teaching his children to practise the positive things of African culture. Love and learn the languages and dialects of Africa. This love will also be fuelled by the appreciation of the sacrifices that were made to free the continent. I can hear African martyrs say from their graves, 'Did we die for this land in vain that those we handed it to might trash and abandon it?' *Love Africa. It's all we've got.*

Second, the Dream must in it embody the Unity of Africa. The Unity of Africa, One Africa, is a major key to Africa's competitiveness among the nations. The Founding Fathers of African Liberation believed passionately in the unity of Africa, and put their actions where their talk was. The fact must not be lost to Africa that if the Continent continues in the present fragmentation, the end will be a shameless re-colonisation, either by respective colonial masters, or by new opportunistic nations. The time is coming when anything that cannot stand for itself will be swallowed.

Third, the Dream must embody a fierce sense of patriotism, identity, distinction, strength, ownership and self-determination. When Africa's generation of Liberators discovered the simple truth, 'We are our own liberators', they defined a dream that must pervade every area of African-ness in the future. Africa must not remain the disabled beggar of the nations, but must now say,

*'We are our own developers, we own our land and resources and the Dream you hear is ours—we own it—we are our own wealth builders, we are our own defenders and simply put, look out world, the Africans have arrived on the block—**we are!***

Self-determination also means Africa must develop its own ideology and systems and not continue to be a monkey performer of systems and ideologies developed by other peoples to suit their own national evolutions. For example, there must be a brand of democracy based on the inclusive African cultural experience so that Africans won't have to slaughter each other every election year as they monkey—perform Western democracy. In the Dream must be a thrust for uncompromising strength in all areas—whether governance, economy, social or military. The misery of the Black Man rose from the fact that he was caught in a competitive era armed with only a bow and arrow while others brandished guns and cannons!

Fourth, the Dream must embody a call to creativeness and enterprise in every field leading to an educated and developed Africa for which no African will ever again be embarrassed before other nations—an Africa Black People will be proud of. Even from the Diaspora of economic, political and intellectual refugees must be a new coming back to Africa. Many will come back physically, but even in those who do not return, hearts, minds and strategies must be placed firmly back on the continent. Africa now has an awesome army of qualified, equipped, skilled and trained human resources all over the world, ready to implement the African Dream. Human resources remain the most important resource Africa has, or will ever have.

Fifth, the Dream must embody in leaders and the people a fervent and unflinching commitment to the dignity, freedom and empowerment of

the African to pursue happiness and to express himself and his ideas freely in every positive, constructive and wholesome way.

A People who have suffered oppression and suppression must forever banish from themselves the folly of abusing one another in any way. The Dream must embody a Godly, humane inclusive and compassionate Africa, driven by such values as Ubuntu that have made Black People the most caring people on earth. The vision to empower its People with essential social services such as health, shelter and education must shine brightly in the Dream.

There are cynical and pessimistic views that mock the power of the Dream on the premise that everything has formed and can never change. Yet history testifies to the fact that no order or kingdom can last forever. One word that is certain in the midst of uncertainties is the word **change.**

As early as the fifth century B.C., the Greek philosopher, Heraclitus of Ephesus, expressed this important principle by issuing the wise saying, *'Panta rei',* *(everything flows).* It's not that long ago since the world looked like it would forever be a Roman world and speak Latin. Then came the Caucasian controlled world of slavery then empire and colonialism—declaring we shall forever speak English, French and German. But things changed, are changing and will change.

One strength that Black People must embrace is to dream dreams that transcend generations—even centuries into the future. Once again, I am reminded of the history of the Jews. It had been literally thousands of years since they as a nation had been dispersed during the first century by Roman military might. As years went by most Jews accepted assimilation in other nations as their destiny-this in spite of the tremendous prejudice they had to endure from other peoples.

Finally, in the nineteenth century, dreamers began to emerge with the dream of a Jewish state in the land of Biblical historical record. Peretz Smolenskin (1842-1885) was a young Russian—born Jew who at a certain time in his short life published the famous paper, *The Eternal People.* In this essay He stated that the Jews, united by the Hebrew language, were a people of high intellect whose ideas would one day bless the world and that they would return to Palestine and bloom there into great world influence.

Another young Jewish intellectual, Theodor Herzl (1860-1904), who had always believed that assimilation was the destiny of the Jews witnessed blatant prejudice in the trial of a Jewish officer in France. His response was to write in 1896 the paper, *'Der Judenstaat'* (The Jewish State), outlining the dream of a future Jewish State in the land of Israel. Though many scoffed at the concept, the dream spread to critical mass and barely fifty years later, the Jewish State was born.

The time of the strength and competitiveness of Africa will surely come. Africa will not seek to enslave or subjugate other people. Yet as surely as his big brothers mocked Joseph "the dreamer" but in the end saw the fruit of his dreams as he ascended the throne of Egypt and fed them all in famine, those who mock Black People and their Dream will one day see their glory and be sustained by their contribution.

So, Dear Africa, dare to dream yet again. Let these words, the words of your Dream be found in the mouths of your children, young and old:

> *Africa, Land endowed to me by Almighty God I pledge my deepest love and commitment to you My heart will always beat faster when I think of you—your oceans, Your forests, your rivers, your lakes, your mountains and valleys*

I pledge my deepest love and loyalty to all your People
For I am one with them, and my Dream is the Dream of One Africa,
    a United Africa—
I will work with my People To build you into one whole again from
    the pieces into which they broke you

You are mine, Africa and I am yours—to defend you, to build you
And yes, to own your resources and draw from them to feed, shelter,
    nurture My children and my People—yes, adorn them, adorn you,
Till we become the envy of the nations who gaze with wonder at our glory

I draw strength from you, Africa, and I will labour to strengthen you And
    enterprise—that within your borders, your people will pursue their
    Dreams, and find happiness, means and dignity so fully in you that
No People will ever again despise or tread them down

Africa, I pledge my allegiance to the Dream of your heroes and martyrs
    That in freedom, a caring justice and African inclusiveness govern
    your People For their price I treasure you—and no matter how far
    I journey,
I will always return to you, and with my gifts embrace and serve my
    People.

Yes Africa, it is time for you to tell the nations,

"Hear this dream which I dreamed—your sheaves stood round about,
and made obeisance to my sheaf."

For, though you seem to be the last born of the nations, yet surely you are their Joseph, you will one day feed them.

Some Of Africa's Heroes, Visionaries And Liberators speak

American all time "The Greatest" world boxing champion who was named the 1999 Sportsman of The Century (Sports Illustrated) and Personality of The Century (BBC). He claimed his African identity by rejecting the slave name Cassius Clay. He is an outspoken fighter for Black people's rights, "Impossible is just a big word thrown around by small men who find it easier to live in the world they've been given than to explore the power they have to change it. Impossible is not a fact. It's an opinion. Impossible is not a declaration. It's a dare. Impossible is potential. Impossible is temporary. Impossible is nothing."

- *"Wars of nations are fought to change maps. But wars of poverty are fought to map change."*
- *"The man who has no imagination has no wings."*

The joy of Independence Day.

Dr Robert Mugabe, Zimbabwe Liberation Leader and first Black President of The Republic of Zimbabwe, surrounded by excited and expectant masses at Liberation Rally in 1979. Black people have great expectations of those who rise to lead them politically.

Acknowledgements

1. Cover Photo
    Extended License, Rufuse Ezekiel Content ID:2179231, *www.fotolia.com*

2. Page 5
    Etnath Easwaran ; Gandhi the Man : How one man changed himself to change the world, Nilgri Press 1973
    Judith M. Brown : Gandhi, Prisoner of Hope. Yale Univ Press 1991

3. Page 13
    Rabbi Hillel was born to a wealthy family in Babylonia, but came to Jerusalem without the financial support of his family and supported himself as a woodcutter. It is said that he lived in such great poverty that he was sometimes unable to pay the admission fee to study *Torah*, and because of him that fee was abolished. He was known for his kindness, his gentleness, and his concern for humanity. One of his most famous sayings, recorded in Pirkei Avot (Ethics of the Fathers, a tractate of the *Mishnah*), is "If I am not for myself, then who will be for me? And if I am only for myself, then what am I? And if not now, when?" The Hillel organization, a network of Jewish college student organizations, is named for him

4. Page 16

   Door of no return : From Wikipedia, The Free Encyclopedia

   The **House of Slaves** (*Maison des Esclaves*) and its **Door of No Return** is a museum and memorial to the *Atlantic slave trade* on tiny *Goree Island*, 3km off the coast of the city of *Dakar, Senegal.* Its museum, opened in 1962 and curated until his death in 2009 by *Boubacar Joseph Ndiaye*, is said to memorialise the final exit point of the *slaves* from *Africa.* Historians differ on how many, if any African slaves were actually held in this building, as well as the relative importance of Goree Island as a point on the Atlantic Slave Trade,[1] but visitors from Africa, Europe and the Americas, along with world leaders, continue to make it an important place to remember the human toll of African slavery.

5. Page 17

   Rudd Concession From Wikipedia, The Free Encyclopedia. This is the treaty by which Cecil Rhodes engineered the colonization of Mashonaland and Matabeleland, now Zimbabwe.

6. Page 18

   From Wikipedia, The Free Encyclopedia

   Example of whites who claimed blacks were not human) Voltaire was a *French Enlightenment* writer, *historian* and *philosopher.* He was a *polygenist*: he believed that each race had separate origins. Voltaire found biblical *mon ogenism* laughable, as he expressed:

   > It is a serious question among them whether the Africans are descended from monkeys or whether the monkeys come from them. Our wise men have said that man was created in the image of God. Now here is a lovely image of the Divine Maker: a flat and black nose with little or hardly any intelligence. A time will doubtless

come when these animals will know how to cultivate the land well, beautify their houses and gardens, and know the paths of the stars: one needs time for everything.[28]

7. Page 19

William Wilberforce: Wilberforce's involvement in the abolition movement was motivated by a desire to put his Christian principles into action and to serve God in public life.[74][75] He and other Evangelicals were horrified by what they perceived was a depraved and unchristian trade, and the greed and avarice of the owners and traders.[75][76] Wilberforce sensed a call from God, writing in a journal entry in 1787 that "God Almighty has set before me two great objects, the suppression of the Slave Trade and the Reformation of Manners [moral values]".[77][78] The conspicuous involvement of Evangelicals in the highly popular anti-slavery movement served to improve the status of a group otherwise associated with the less popular campaigns against vice and immorality.[79] From Wikipedia, the free encyclopedia.)

8. Page 20

Napoleon Bonaparte (French: *Napoléon Bonaparte* 15 August 1769 – 5 May 1821) was a French military and political leader who rose to prominence during the latter stages of the *French Revolution* and its associated *wars* in Europe. As **Napoleon I**, he was *Emperor of the French* from 1804 to 1815. His legal reform, the *Napoleonic Code*, has been a major influence on many *civil law* jurisdictions worldwide, but he is best remembered for his role in the wars led against France by a series of coalitions, the so-called *Napoleonic Wars*. He established hegemony over most of continental Europe and sought to spread the ideals of the French Revolution, while consolidating an *imperial monarchy* which restored aspects of the deposed *Ancien Régime*. Due to his success in these wars, often against numerically superior enemies, he is generally regarded as one of the greatest military commanders of all time, and his campaigns are studied at military academies worldwide.[1]

Abraham Lincoln (February 12, 1809 – April 15, 1865) was the *16th President of the United States*, serving from March 1861 until *his assassination in April 1865*. Lincoln led the United States through its greatest constitutional, military, and moral crises—the *American Civil War*—preserving the *Union*, abolishing slavery, strengthening the national government and modernizing the economy. Reared in a poor family on the *western frontier*, Lincoln was self-educated, and became a country lawyer, a *Whig Party leader, Illinois state legislator* during the 1830s, and a one-term member of the *United States House of Representatives* during the 1840s.

The **Battle of Waterloo** was fought on Sunday, 18 June 1815 near *Waterloo* in present-day *Belgium*, then part of the *United Kingdom of the Netherlands*. An *Imperial French* army under the command of *Emperor Napoleon* was defeated by the armies of the *Seventh Coalition*, comprising an Anglo-Allied army under the command of the *Duke of Wellington* combined with a *Prussian* army under the command of *Gebhard von Blücher*. It was the culminating battle of the *Waterloo Campaign* and Napoleon's last. The defeat at Waterloo ended his rule as Emperor of the French, marking the end of his *Hundred Days* return from exile.

9. Page 20
    Names of some African Liberation movements: Umkhonto we Sizwe: Meaning the Spear of the Nation – Military wing of the African National Congress of South Africa
    ZANLA:-The Zimbabwe African National Liberation Army : military wing of ZANU, the Zimbabwe African National Union

ZIPRA – The Zimbabwe People's Revolutionary Army ; military wing of ZAPU, the Zimbabwe African People's Union

SWAPO – South West African People's Organisation: the organisation that executed Namibia's war of liberation and is the ruling party in Namibia.

10. Page 20

Bantu Steven Biko {see page 101); Malcom X (see page 107); Marcus Garvey (see page 60); Kwame Nkrumah (see page 100)

11. Page 27

Steve Biko quote : From a speech delivered in Cape Town, 1971.

12. Page 27

"Every time I hear the crack of a whip . . ." Lyrics from Slave Driver by *Bob Marley & The Wailers*

13. Page 34

'Ask not what your country . . . ' US President JF Kennedy, speech delivered at his inauguration, Washington, DC January 20, 1961.

14. Page 35

'Ubuntu' a Zulu term, "is an age-old African expression for humaneness for caring, sharing and being in harmony with all of creation. As an ideal it promotes cooperation between individuals, cultures and nations".

15. Page 35

"weapons of mass deception" is a pejorative expression used by some people to describe U.S. President *George W. Bush*'s claim that *Saddam Hussein* possessed *weapons of mass destruction* as justification for the *war on Iraq*.

In Africa the expression is used to describe propagandist media articles or statements. *http://en.wikipedia.org/wiki/Weapons_of_Mass_Deception*

16. Pages 38 to 48

    Pictures of The African Holocaust And Other Pictures

    Wikimedia Commons, the free media repository. Public Domain

    Creative Commons Attribution/Share-Alike License: Wero Ishango bone with the numbers: 19, 17, 13 and 11 / 7, 5, 5, 10, 8, 4, 6 and 3 / 9, 19, 21 and 11. http://www. corbisimages. sharpeville-massacre

    UNESCO ASPnet Projects, The Middle Passage, Kristina Pettersen. Triangular Slave Trade, Eric Hager.

    History of Slavery, Slavery in Africa, Atlantic Slave Trade, From Wikipedia, the free encyclopedia, *en.wikipedia.org/wiki/History_of_slavery*

17. Page 43

    From Wikipedia, the free encyclopedia

    Africa Fact. Largest solar energy capacity:

    Many African countries receive on average 325 days per year of bright sunlight.[9] This gives solar power the potential to bring energy to virtually any location in Africa without the need for expensive large scale grid level infrastructural developments. The distribution of solar resources across Africa is fairly uniform, with more than 80 percent of their landscape receiving almost 2000 *kW·h* per square meter per year. A recent study indicates that a solar generating facility covering just 0.3% of the area comprising North Africa could supply all of the energy required by the European Union.[10]

18. Page 53

    Charles Kingsley 1819-1875 from the second of his letters to the Chartists

19. Page 63

    Holy Bible, KJV Genesis 11 v 6

20. Page 74

    Kwame Nrumah advocated the united states of Africa 9 (Wikipedia)

21. Page 91

    Holy Bible, KJV Deuteronomy 8

22. Page 95

    Africa's Greatest Entrepreneurs A book about Africa's business success stories
    "Until lions learn to write, hunters will tell their history for them" Review
    by David Fick

    www.mmemedia.co.za/age.pdf.

    www.blackentrepreneurprofile.com lists a number of successful Black
    Entrepreneurs on several continents

23. Pages 100-108

    Pictures of Africa's Past And Present Visionaries, Wikipedia, the free
    encyclopaedia

    "No Land! No House! No Vote!" Campaign, Wikipedia, the free
    encyclopaedia

    http://en.wikipedia.org/wiki/

24. Page 105

    Africa Fact—User: Globalecon/African Diamond Mines

    From Wikipedia, the free encyclopedia

    African diamond mines produce approximately 50% of the world's *diamond*
    supply. Today, Africa is said to have mined more than 1.9 billion carats of
    diamonds at an estimated $158 billion in US dollars. This has earned Africa

the title of the largest diamond industry in the world ahead of *Russia* and *Canada*.

25. Page 116

   From Wikipedia, the free encyclopedia

   Malawians in Europe largely reside in the *United Kingdom* since Malawi was a former colony of Britain. Many of the Malawians in the UK are health workers, particularly doctors. There are currently more than 250 Malawian doctors in *Manchester*, which means that there are more Malawian doctors in Manchester than in the entire country of Malawi.[13][14][15]

26. Page 130

   2007–08 Kenyan Crisis, Wikipedia, the free encyclopedia

   Riots erupted in Kenya after Kibaki was declared re-elected as President in the 2007 Presidential Elections. Certain opposition supporters, angered by alleged electoral manipulation by President Kibaki, allegedly incited civil unrest. The unrest involved ethnic violence between members of different tribes, particularly between the Kikuyu and the Kalenjin.[73] Hundreds of people died. Eventually, a power-sharing agreement, according to which Kibaki would remain President and Odinga would gain the new post of Prime Minister, was reached in late February 2008, and a coalition government, with an equal number of ministers for the PNU and the ODM, was named in April.

27. Page 137

   Young Joseph speaking to his brothers, The Holy Bible: King James Version. 2000. Genesis 37 vs 6

28. Page 151

The *Marshall Plan* and U.S. troop presence in Germany left a legacy of *cooperation* between both nations, politically, economically, and militarily. At the beginning of the occupation of post war Germany, the Allies started dismantling the remnants of German industries. The Allies confiscated significant values of German *patents, copyrights* and *trademarks*.

29. Page 138

Mau Mau Uprising Compensation Bid Begins Against The British Government By Kenyan Victims Of Alleged Brutality. *http://www.zimbio. com/pictures* John Nottingham, a former District Officer in the Colonial Service stands outside the High Court on April 7, 2011 in London, England. Mr Nottingham is a witness for four Kenyans who are taking the British Government to court over allegations that they were tortured during the Mau Mau uprising when Britain was the colonial power. They claim they were assaulted between 1952 and 1961. Kenya gained independence in 1963.—04-06 16:00:00—Source: Peter Macdiarmid/Getty Images Europe)

30. Page 149

Acres of Diamonds by Russell Conwell

31. Page 159

Zanu-PF leader, Robert Mugabe arrives in Highfields to address a pre-election rally in 1979. Next to him are much younger, now late Army General Solomon Mujuru (centre) and current Government Minister Emmerson Mnangagwa (right) The Herald, Zimbabwe 1979

www.ingramcontent.com/pod-product-compliance
Lightning Source LLC
Chambersburg PA
CBHW031321290526
45784CB00014B/581